available at

Editor's Picks

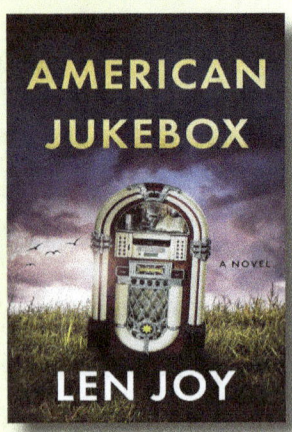

American Jukebox
LEN JOY

A beautifully written, character-driven story that masterfully explores family, identity, and resilience with heartfelt emotion and relatable depth.

Paperback: £12.95

https://tinyurl.com/mwutswhk

A Memory of Fictions
LEONCE GAITER

A daring, lyrical masterpiece—Gaiter's voice is unforgettable, weaving raw honesty and poetic brilliance into a fiercely original narrative.

Paperback: £12.67

https://tinyurl.com/yckr4v8u

LIT
MARK ANTHONY

LIT is an exceptional blend of suspense, originality, and emotional depth, delivering a thrilling and unforgettable reading experience.

Paperback: £13.24

https://tinyurl.com/47v5wjsa

Henry's Chapel
GRAHAM GUEST

Innovative, intellectually daring, and structurally ambitious, Henry's Chapel challenges conventional storytelling with its unique metafictional approach and thought-provoking narrative framework.

Paperback: £13.99

https://tinyurl.com/2v5uatte

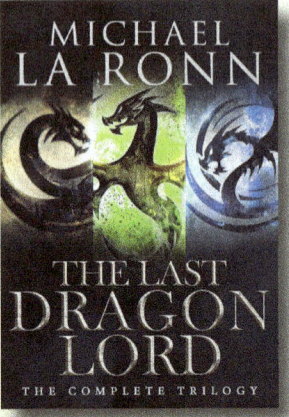

The Last Dragon Lord
MICHAEL LA RONN

A masterfully written dark fantasy, The Last Dragon Lord captivates with its rich world-building, complex antihero, and gripping tension.

Kindle: £8.99

https://tinyurl.com/2bph6jed

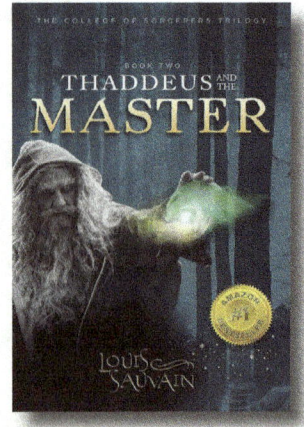

Thaddeus and the Master
LOUIS SAUVAIN

Rich world-building, compelling characters, imaginative challenges, and heartfelt camaraderie make Thaddeus and the Master an enthralling fantasy masterpiece.

Paperback: £17.22

https://tinyurl.com/4rbb79xh

Plagued Lands
NIKKI BROOKE

Plagued Lands enthrals with its thrilling plot, heartfelt relationships, and a courageous heroine, making it an unmissable dystopian gem.

Paperback: £12.99

https://tinyurl.com/msx3xww2

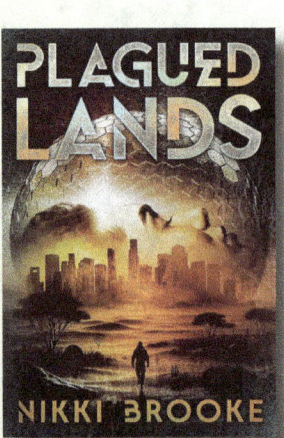

Thurkill's Rebellion
PAUL BERNARDI

A gripping, action-packed historical adventure with rich detail, compelling characters, and intense battle scenes. A must-read for medieval fiction fans!

Paperback: £8.99

https://tinyurl.com/mpr35ytt

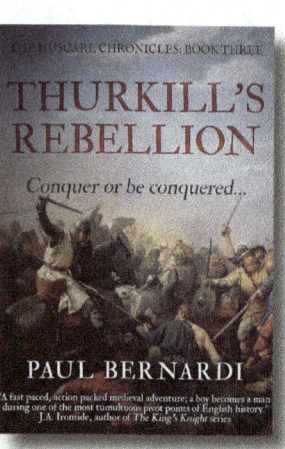

Your Gateway to Endless Stories

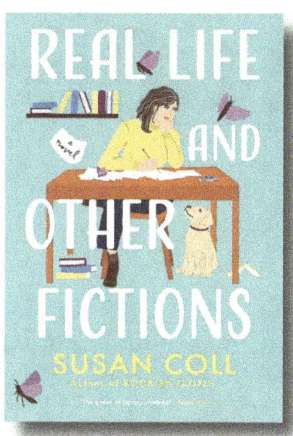

Real Life and Other Fictions
SUSAN COLL

Witty, heartfelt, and wonderfully eccentric—Real Life and Other Fictions is a captivating blend of mystery, humour, and self-discovery.

Paperback: £6.89

https://tinyurl.com/yc7c2t46

UnAuthored Letters
TARA C. ALLRED

A gripping, emotionally rich psychological thriller with masterful storytelling, compelling characters, and an unpredictable mystery that keeps readers enthralled until the end.

Paperback: £11.13

https://tinyurl.com/3uanerz8

The Moving Blade
MICHAEL PRONKO

A gripping, atmospheric thriller with rich cultural depth, sharp plotting, and compelling characters. The Moving Blade is a masterfully crafted crime novel.

Paperback: £19.99

https://tinyurl.com/4rm468dt

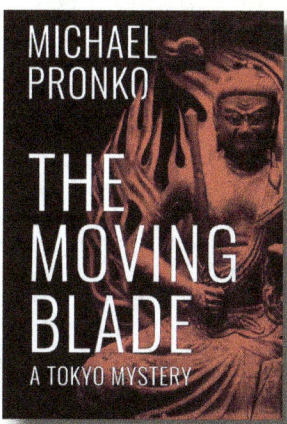

My AfroRican State of Soul
LUCAS RIVERA

A powerful, poetic masterpiece—raw, rhythmic, and deeply moving. Rivera's voice resonates with authenticity, bridging generations through identity, struggle, and art.

Paperback: £15.84

https://tinyurl.com/mttjpjfb

The Empath's Survival Guide
JUDITH ORLOFF

Insightful, empowering, and deeply validating—The Empath's Survival Guide is an essential resource for sensitive souls seeking balance, resilience, and self-acceptance.

Paperback: £11.35

https://tinyurl.com/mry6p2cp

Heroes of Reighja
JIM GILL

An enthralling tale of mystery, adventure, and rich world-building, Heroes of Reighja captivates with its emotional depth and intrigue.

Kindle: £22.79

https://tinyurl.com/4wsc8z9a

Murder by the Brush
S.E. BABIN

S.E. Babin crafts a delightful, witty mystery filled with heart, humour, and an unforgettable cast of living and ghostly characters.

Kindle: £0.77

https://tinyurl.com/2aaakaes

The Angel and the Amazing Life of Maggie Love
C.R. FABIS

A masterful blend of mystery and morality, Fabis delivers a thought-provoking tale that captivates with complex characters and powerful storytelling.

Paperback: £12.41

https://tinyurl.com/547pthb8

VOICES OF LITERATURE

What's INSIDE

 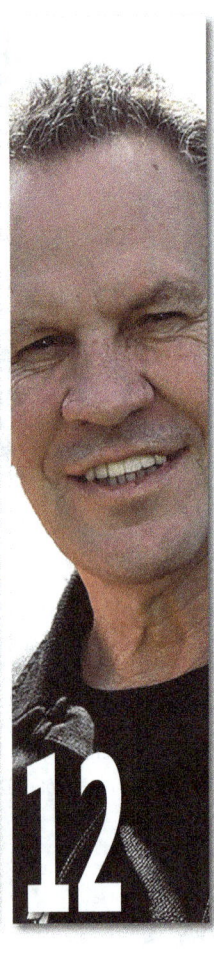    

10 **12** **14** **16** **18** **20**

DEBBIE MIRZA
Illuminates the Healing Path After Narcissistic Abuse

RICHARD PHILLIPS
Explores the Human Cost of Power Through Science, Magic, and Military Precision

MARIEKE LEXMOND
Weaves Enchantment and Intrigue into Fantasy Worlds

SHERRI L. DODD
From Fitness To Fiction Through Grief And Magick

PENN FAWN
Exploring Death, Hope, And Horror Across Realms

ILUTA SUTRA
Inspires Through Her Writing on Love, Healing and Forgiveness

 42 Kiki Howell

 46 Nelle L'AMOUR

Author Interviews

22
GARY TREW
Shares the Healing Power of Humour and the Weight of Truth

24
SUSAN ROWLAND
Redefining Marginalised Women As Heroes

30
ALMAN D GUIDE
Navigating Mystical Traditions

32
CARMEN AMATO
Exploring the Detective Emilia Cruz Series

34
STEPHANIE COWELL
A Journey Through Creativity, Romance, and Historical Truths

36
DARYL BANNER
Exploring Love, Identity, and Self-Acceptance Through Character-Driven Stories and Humour

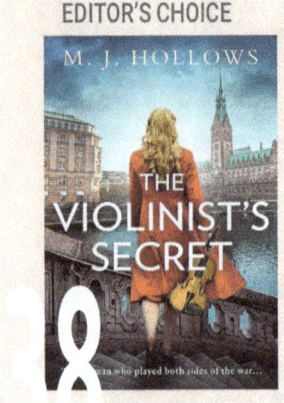

EDITOR'S CHOICE

NOVEL • STORY • LITERATURE

THE VIOLINIST'S SECRET
by M.J. Hollows

WHITE FIRE
by Laurie Bell

EDITOR'S CHOICE highlights exceptional books, offering insights to guide readers in discovering their next great read.

What's INSIDE
Issue 56 - 2025

STAR INTERVIEW

ELIZABETH MAGILL — 48

50 CECILE CHONG

52 SIENNA MARTZ

26

COVER

JILL SANDERS
Insights Into Romance, Trust And Second Chances

The Queen Of Romance, Spinning Timeless Tales That Touch Hearts Across The Globe

55 DR SHIRIN LAKHANI — Inspires Change in Wellness, Aesthetic Medicine, and Intimate Health

58 DR IVONA IGERC

60 CHARMAINE CHOW

BEAUTY

Scan QR to read online or updated issue.

8 || *Reader's House*

From the Editor

Welcome to the 56th issue of *Reader's House*! We are thrilled to bring you yet another collection of captivating literary discoveries, insightful interviews, and inspiring stories to ignite your imagination and enrich your bookshelf.

This month, our *Star Interview* shines brightly on Jill Sanders, a New York Times, USA Today, and internationally bestselling author known for her timeless tales of romance, trust, and second chances. With over 100 books spanning genres like Sweet Contemporary Romance, Romantic Suspense, Western Romance, and Paranormal Romance, Jill's novels have touched hearts across the globe. Her ability to blend heartfelt characters, vivid settings, and universal themes of love and resilience makes her a true luminary in the literary world. In this exclusive feature, Jill shares her creative process, the inspirations behind her compelling characters, and the magic that fuels her storytelling. Whether you're a longtime fan or new to her works, her journey as an author is sure to inspire.

But Jill Sanders isn't the only author we celebrate in this issue. We've had the honor of interviewing a lineup of exceptional literary voices whose works span across genres and themes—each bringing their unique perspectives and talents to the literary world. Debbie Mirza illuminates the healing path after narcissistic abuse with her writings, while Richard Phillips explores the human cost of power through a masterful blend of science, magic, and precision. Marieke Lexmond enchants readers with fantasy worlds rich in intrigue, and Sherri L. Dodd takes us from fitness to fiction, weaving stories layered with personal journeys. Penn Fawn delves into themes of death, hope, and horror, while Iluta Sutra inspires with expressions of love, healing, and forgiveness.

Further enriching this issue are interviews with Gary Trew, Susan Rowland, Alman D Guide, Carmen Amato, Stephanie Cowell, Daryl Banner, Kiki Howell, and Nelle L'amour. Each of these authors brings their creative magic to the pages of literature—whether they're redefining marginalized women as heroes, navigating mystical traditions, exploring the depths of human relationships, or blending humor with history. Their works remind us of literature's boundless ability to transport, challenge, and connect us.

As always, this issue's *Editor's Picks* highlights extraordinary books for avid readers. From thrilling dystopias like Nikki Brooke's *Plagued Lands* to captivating historical adventures like Paul Bernardi's *Thurkill's Rebellion*, and from emotional literary masterpieces like Leonce Gaiter's *A Memory of Fictions* to innovative narratives like Graham Guest's *Henry's Chapel*, these selections promise unforgettable reading experiences.

Finally, we invite you to immerse yourself in the diversity of voices featured in *Voices of Literature*. Whether it's Carmen Amato's gripping detective series, Stephanie Cowell's blend of creativity and historical truths, or Susan Rowland's redefinition of women as heroes, each interview offers a glimpse into the minds of authors who reshape perspectives and ignite dialogue.

In today's fast-paced and ever-evolving world, the stories we tell—and the ones we embrace—carry the power to inspire change, foster understanding, and awaken joy. We hope this issue of *Reader's House Magazine* serves as your gateway to endless stories and discoveries.

Thank you for being part of our community. As always, we look forward to sharing the journey of storytelling with you. Let the turn of every page remind you of the magic that literature holds.

PUBLISHER: READER'S HOUSE MAGAZINE, A Subsidiary of NewYox Media Group. 200 Suite 134-146 Curtain Road, EC2A 3AR London, United Kingdom t: +44 79 3847 8420 editor@readershouse.co.uk II http://readershouse.co.uk II http://newyox.media
EDITORIAL: Anna Harlowe Editor-in-Chief, Dan Peters, Managing Editor, Ben Alan, Art Editor, Z. Robers, Content Editor.
CONTRIBUTORS Claudine D. Reyes, Mickey Mikkelson, Andrea Piacquadio, Adrian T. Cheng, Donna Schim, Jon Allo, Tim Halloran, Oleg Magni, Amir SeilSepour, Bill Youngblood, Jetty Stutzman, Jimmy Choo, Peter Filinovich.

We assume no responsibility for unsolicited manuscripts or art materials provided from our contributors. All content in this magazine is © copyrighted to NewYox Media. Unauthorized reproduction, distribution, or transmission of any part of this publication without written permission from the NewYox Media is strictly prohibited.

Bestselling Author and Coach Shares Insight Through Books Meditations and Music

DEBBIE MIRZA

Illuminates the Healing Path After Narcissistic Abuse

BY DAN PETERS | LONDON

Debbie Mirza. A name synonymous with hope, healing, and profound transformation in the realm of emotional recovery and personal empowerment. Her work has touched the lives of countless individuals across the globe, providing insight, solace, and strength to those navigating the aftermath of covert narcissistic abuse. Through her international bestseller, *The Covert Passive-Aggressive Narcissist*, Debbie has shed light on a subject previously shrouded in misunderstanding, offering clarity and truth to survivors seeking answers.

With over 9000 glowing reviews, her words have been embraced by readers, listeners, and mental health professionals alike, cementing her position as a leading voice on this crucial topic. Yet, Debbie's influence extends far beyond the pages of her books. Her holistic approach incorporates guided meditations, music, coaching, and courses, all designed to aid individuals in reclaiming their worth, rediscovering their inner strength, and finding the peace they deserve.

In our conversation with Debbie, we delve into the stories behind her transformative works, including *Worthy of Love* and her upcoming addition to the series, which promises to explore the most essential element of healing. Join us as we uncover the inspiration behind her writings, the impact of her meditations and music, and her heartfelt advice for aspiring authors. Debbie's journey is a testament to resilience, empathy, and the power of softening the sharp edges of trauma through compassion and understanding. Prepare to be inspired.

In 'The Covert Passive-Aggressive Narcissist', you explore subtle forms of abuse. What inspired you to delve into this lesser-known aspect of narcissism?

I began researching this form of narcissistic abuse after realizing I had been with a covert narcissist for many years and had not recognized the traits. At that time, most of the information out there was about the more well-known overt narcissist, so it was difficult to find accurate information on this more insidious, subtle form of narcissism.

After years of research and working on my own healing I was at a stronger and clearer place where I could help others, so I decided to write the book I needed all those years ago, so other survivors would have an easier time finding the answers they needed and deserved. I determined to make this book the most accurate, thorough, and helpful book out there.

I interviewed over one-hundred people, including therapists, coaches, and survivors who had experienced different types of relationships with covert narcissists, from parents to spouses or partners, friends, family members, and work colleagues to help this be a well-rounded book, so everyone, no matter what type of relationship they had been in, would be able to receive clarity.

'Worthy of Love' offers a restorative path post-abuse. How does this book build upon the foundation laid in your previous work?

There are profound and life-altering effects that come from being involved with a covert narcissist. It is common for survivors to experience chronic health issues, exhaustion, low self-esteem, low self-worth and difficulty trusting themselves and others. Many feel alone, isolated, judged, and misunderstand. Fear and anxiety become a daily experience after years of being in a fight, fight, or freeze state in order to survive the abuse.

My book, Worthy of Love, gives a much-needed roadmap for people to come back to their whole selves again, to heal from what they have been through, and be able to move forward with their life with more self-love, confidence, clarity, peace, and strength.

Your personal experiences have deeply influenced your writing. How did your journey shape the narratives in your books?

Because I have experienced this type of abuse throughout my life, in different kinds of relationships, I care deeply about other's who have been through similar experiences because I know how it feels and how it affects us.

I am a tender-hearted, sensitive, and empathetic person, and with the knowledge and wisdom I now have after years of studying and working on my own healing, I have a drive and a passion to help people see through the lies they received about themselves, and see the truth of how valuable and important they are.

You've created guided meditations and music alongside your books. How do these mediums complement your written work in aiding healing?

Music and meditations are powerful mediums to help us calm our nervous systems and rewrite the false beliefs we have received from those who have projected untruths onto us.

For example, one of the meditations I created is called, Rewriting False Messages from Narcissists and Toxic People. I gathered the common messages we receive from narcissists, and speak to these in the meditation, so in a relaxed state, people's minds can receive the truth. This not only brings calm to the body and mind, but it helps rewrite the wrongs.

Music, for me, has been a powerful tool that helps remind me what love really feels like. Years ago, during a deeply healing year, I wrote songs I needed to hear and recorded them so others could hear them too. I entitled the album, Soul Rising, to represent the path of the survivor.

Many therapists recommend your books. What feedback have you received from mental health professionals about your approach?

I have received so many letters of gratitude from therapists. It has been extraordinary. They will often tell me that they were also with covert narcissists for decades, and even with their training did not recognize the traits.

Many have said they believe my book should be required reading in universities for students training to be future therapists. They have made me aware that people who are currently in school to become a therapist have very brief training about narcissistic personality disorder, and no education on the covert type.

I am grateful for the ones who have done

Debbie Mirza, bestselling author and coach, explores the lasting impact of covert narcissistic abuse and offers compassionate, restorative tools for survivors to reclaim their voice, worth, and emotional well-being.

Debbie Mirza's *The Covert Passive Aggressive Narcissist* is a must-read for anyone seeking clarity on hidden narcissistic abuse. This insightful guide explains covert narcissism traits, manipulation tactics, and emotional damage caused. With real-life examples and a healing roadmap, it empowers readers to reclaim happiness and rebuild their lives. Highly educational and transformative.

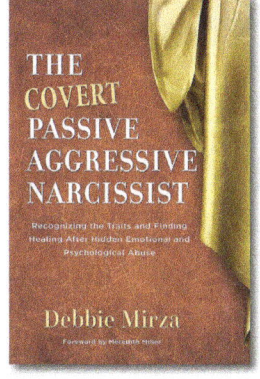

their own independent research so they can truly help survivors.

Your online courses address parenting with a covert narcissist ex. What key challenges do these courses help individuals navigate?

When you are coparenting and the other parent of the children is a covert narcissist, you are dealing with a tremendous amount that others who have not been through this have no way of understanding.

A narcissist will do all they can to make your life and the life of their children extraordinarily difficult. The way they treat their children, and the other parent is unfathomable and deeply disturbing.

These parents need a tremendous amount of support and understanding. The rules, the advice for them, is much different than for those co-parenting with someone who is not a narcissist.

You're currently working on the final book in your series on healing after narcissistic abuse. Can you share what readers might expect from this upcoming work?

In my final book I will be speaking about the most important element to healing after narcissistic abuse. It is such an important topic I felt it needed its own book, dedicated to this one topic.

I am so excited for survivors to be able to have this book. It's unlike anything I've seen before.

What advice would you offer to aspiring authors aiming to write about personal healing and transformation?

I would encourage them to consider writing their book as if they were writing it to themself, to that part of their heart that needs to hear the beautiful words they will bring forth. Try not to be impressive. Try not to prove anything to others. Give the words space to flow through you in their own time. And know that you are brave. Putting anything into the world takes tremendous courage.

> *I decided to write the book I needed all those years ago."*

Debbie Mirza

Debbie Mirza, bestselling author and coach, offers guidance to those recovering from covert emotional abuse.

From Alien Tech to Ancient Prophecy, His Stories Redefine the Sci-Fi and Fantasy Landscape

RICHARD PHILLIPS

Explores the Human Cost of Power Through Science, Magic, and Military Precision

BY Z. ROBERTS | NEW YORK

Richard Phillips, a masterful storyteller and visionary author, continues to captivate the imaginations of readers with his incredible ability to blend cutting-edge science, timeless themes, and deeply human characters. As the creator of bestselling series such as *The Rho Agenda*, *The Rho Agenda Inception*, *The Rho Agenda Assimilation*, and *The Endarian Prophecy,* Richard has firmly established himself as a titan within the realms of science fiction and fantasy. His works, pulsating with heart-pounding action, philosophical depth, and intricate world-building, stand as a testament to his skill and dedication to his craft.

In this issue, we delve into the mind of the brilliant creator behind these enthralling universes. With a foundation rooted in a distinguished military career and a profound understanding of physics, Richard has an unparalleled ability to ground his expansive narratives in scientific plausibility while crafting characters who wrestle with the same vulnerabilities, doubts, and hopes that we all do. From the advanced alien technologies of *The Rho Agenda* to the mysticism and ancient magic of *The Endarian Prophecy*, his stories provide a perfect tapestry of intrigue, innovation, and emotion.

This year, the literary world eagerly anticipates the May 2025 release of Richard's latest offering, *The Ripper's Son*. Building on *The Rho Agenda's* legacy, this new novel introduces a fresh protagonist whose bioengineered abilities collide with the rise of sentient AIs, promising yet another spellbinding exploration of humanity's future in the face of technological evolution. Whether you are a long-time devotee of his work or discovering his writing for the first time, Richard Phillips' unique genius is sure to leave you inspired, entertained, and profoundly moved.

It is both an honour and a privilege to share with you this in-depth interview with an author whose boundless imagination and meticulous expertise continue to shape the landscape of speculative fiction. Prepare to journey behind the scenes of his creative process and immerse yourself in the mind of a storyteller who boldly redefines the limits of literary possibility.

What initially inspired you to blend military experience with science fiction storytelling in your novels?

Serving in the military at West Point and then as a U.S. Army Officer provided me with a first-hand understanding of the discipline, camaraderie, and personal challenges associated with war, deployments, and family separation. Technology is changing modern warfare and impacting everyday life in such a major way that this is a prime moment in history to glimpse ahead at what is coming our way in the near future. Everything from artificial intelligence, nano-technology, to our very understanding of the underlying rules that govern our universe are being questioned. Exploring that impact on my characters is what I call fun.

How did your background in physics and time at Los Alamos influence the scientific concepts in The Rho Agenda?

Working at the Los Alamos and Lawrence Livermore National Laboratories immersed me in explorations of physics that blur our conceptions of theory and the underlying reality. Conversations about quantum mechanics, the duality of particles and waves, and the computational models we construct to simulate them were part of my daily life. That experience grounded my Rho Agenda series in science that is not only plausible but may soon be feasible. My physics background enabled me to weave complex quantum theory concepts with artificial intelligence into the evolving story in a readily understandable way that allows imagination to take flight.

Richard Phillips discusses the inspirations behind his bestselling series, the intersection of science and fantasy, complex characters, and the highly anticipated release of his newest novel, The Ripper's Son.

In developing the Endarian Prophecy series, what drew you to the themes of prophecy and ancient magic?

Born in Roswell, New Mexico, I had an intense curiosity about the concept of alien life and the questions "Are we alone in this universe?" and if not, "What are those other worlds like?" I grew up loving the works of Heinlein, Bradbury, Scott Card, and Tolkien. My love of fantasy was similar to my fascination with science fiction. Both explore mystical concepts that I use to force my characters through extraordinarily difficult circumstances. To me, the best stories are those where the main characters find themselves in situations that would cause ordinary people to give up. They must adapt or perish. Satisfying novels revolve around this necessity for change.

How do you balance fast-paced action with deeper philosophical or ethical questions in your writing?

Action drives my stories and is the gristmill that applies pressure to my characters. It forces them to make tough choices that expose their true values, whether they believe those to be their true values or not. I layer questions about loyalty, sacrifice, selfishness, and the price of power into every confrontation. It's not just about survival. It's about how survival and how the losses the characters suffer along the way change them. I often use narrative or dialogue to explore character philosophy and beliefs, but character actions reveal what really lies beneath the surface.

The Rho Agenda explores the impact of alien technology on teenagers—why did you choose young protagonists for such high-stakes narratives?

I love coming of age stories because each of us has experienced our own version of how those struggles mold us into the people we eventually become. In The Rho Agenda series, Heather McFarland and the twins, Mark and Jennifer Smythe, embody the normal teen challenges plus the weight of having been altered by an alien encounter. Many of us wonder; if I could just go back in time and change my actions during this or that traumatic event, would I do it? The answer depends on how you feel about your current situation. If there are good things in your life that you would never give up, then the probable answer is NO. To change one thing might change everything. But as a young person, every failure is tragic, every joyous experience is radiant. Lack of previous experience amplifies everything. That's what makes this type of story so much fun.

What inspired you to create heroes who aren't invincible, but deeply human?

Heroes who never fail are boring. Humans, or aliens for that matter, are interesting because they are flawed and vulnerable. Whether it's Jack 'The Ripper' Gregory in my Rho Agenda series, or Rob Gregory in my new Rho Agenda novel, The Ripper's Son, my protagonists face inner demons every bit as formidable as their enemies. Their struggles give their victories and their lives meaning. In the most powerful science fiction and fantasy stories, the moments when our heroes fail are the gut punches that leave us cheering for them to rise up and continue the fight.

How much of your own worldview and values do you embed into characters like Jack Gregory or Lorness Carol?

I avoid having my characters preach my personal philosophy. However, my belief about what makes a hero, including how I define honorable and dishonorable deeds, makes its way into the persona of both my heroes and my villains. In my Rho Agenda series,

Bestselling author Richard Phillips, whose work blends physics, action, and philosophy, captured at his writing studio in Phoenix, Arizona.

Jack Gregory's struggle against his inner demon mirrors my belief that people aren't defined by their worst mistakes, but by their determination to become better. In the Endarian Prophecy series, Lorness Carol Rafel embodies resilience and moral clarity—values I deeply respect. I'm drawn to protagonists who doubt themselves, but who ultimately find the courage to do what's right, even when the cost is high. That's the kind of hero I can believe in.

What's the most rewarding part of world-building across multiple series?

The most rewarding part of this experience for me is seeing the worlds I build evolve, turning corners that I never completely envision when I start writing the series. Every choice I make with technology or with magic has unintended consequences that reveal themselves as the books and series progress. These layers gradually become a living, breathing world that my readers and I get to experience together. Whether it's the fragmented superintelligence that governs our world in The Ripper's Son, the nine ancient magics of The Endarian Prophecy, or the alien physics in The Rho Agenda, I enjoy seeing my readers debate theories, spot hidden connections, and become emotionally invested in worlds that evolved during the telling.

How do you keep scientific elements accessible to readers who aren't scientists?

Characters drive every story. Science underlays the rules of the world, but it's the emotions that the readers can only experience through my characters that propel the story forward. When it comes to complex topics like artificial intelligence, quantum entanglement, or nanotechnology, I show how they impact individual lives, whether that be saving or destroying. I keep the technical jargon to a minimum. It already feels like we are living in a science fiction world. Pushing the boundaries in my stories should spark wonder without requiring a physics degree to enjoy.

What inspired your latest novel, The Ripper's Son, and how does it build on the world you've created in The Rho Agenda?

The Ripper's Son expands the universe of The Rho Agenda by focusing on Rob Gregory, the son of Jack 'The Ripper' Gregory. Rob possesses a unique ability to sense and manipulate electronics through a bio-engineered interface that feels like an extension of his own nervous system. I wanted to explore how that gift—both blessing and curse—puts him at the heart of a new war, this time between competing self-aware AIs. The book combines action, emotional stakes, and high-concept technology in a way that honors the legacy of my original Rho Agenda series while launching a fresh, character-driven conflict for a new generation of readers. This world needs a savior. Only one question remains: Can Robert Brice Gregory bear the cost?

> *Technology is changing modern warfare and impacting everyday life…this is a prime moment in history to glimpse ahead."*

Richard Phillips

Blending Magic, Family and Self-Discovery

MARIEKE LEXMOND

Weaves Enchantment and Intrigue into Fantasy Worlds

BY BEN ALAN | LONDON

Marieke Lexmond stands as an extraordinary force within the realm of fantasy literature, captivating readers with her award-winning creations wrapped in magic, mystery, and emotional depth. A writer of boundless imagination and a solitary witch with an unyielding connection to the mystical, Lexmond has charmed audiences worldwide with *The Madigan Chronicles*, a series resplendent with enchanted worlds, complex characters, and tales that intertwine the supernatural with the deeply human. Her ability to transport readers, whether through the bustling vibrance of New Orleans, the wild beauty of Ireland, or the elemental power of Greenland, is nothing short of magical.

Having begun her storytelling journey in the realm of film, Marieke honed her artistic vision before turning to the written word, where she masterfully conjures immersive narratives laced with themes of family, self-discovery, and resilience. Titles such as *The Wand*, *The Cup*, and *The Queen of Fairy* remind us why Lexmond is a master of magical realism—layering vivid imagery, intricate world-building, and gripping familial dynamics throughout her works. Through her stories, she offers readers an exploration of what it means to embrace one's true self while blending fairy-tale wonder with modern dilemmas.

In this issue's feature interview, Marieke Lexmond opens the door to her creative world. From the influence of her cherished landscapes to the deep bonds within the Madigan family, and her collaborative magic with tarot artist Nicole Ruijgrok, she reflects on the sparks of inspiration behind her award-winning series. Readers and aspiring authors alike are sure to find not only inspiration but also wisdom in the words of this brilliant author whose storytelling feels like an enchanting spell come to life. Prepare to be transported.

How did your experiences living in New Orleans and the west coast of Ireland influence the setting and atmosphere in The Queen of Fairy?

Both places feed my writer's soul in their own way. The energy and atmosphere of New Orleans flow straight into the Madigan's bar, Under the Witches Hat—that city's vibrance, its magical and mysterious undercurrent, and the lively ambiance all live there. Ireland, on the other hand, grounds me in nature. It's where I connect deeply with the land, and that connection shapes the world of Fairy. I'm constantly taking pictures—drawn to texture, light, and the way nature shifts—and that visual inspiration helps me write what Fairy looks and feels like.

In The Wand, you weave elemental powers and teenage trauma—what inspired Ceri's journey as Keeper of the Land?

I think part of life's journey is discovering who you are—and allowing yourself to fully be that person. Society puts so much pressure on us to fit into certain molds, to behave a certain way. Through Ceri, I wanted to explore that struggle, and show how liberating it can be to

Marieke Lexmond delves into her creative process, shares the magic behind The Madigan Chronicles, and discusses inspiration from landscapes, family dynamics, and the role of tarot in her storytelling.

embrace your true self, even when the path is incredibly difficult.

The Cup transports readers to Greenland—what drew you to that remote location and how did it shape Luna and Freya's character arcs?

I made a documentary in Greenland, A Greenland Story, and was deeply inspired by the raw, elemental energy of the landscape and the generosity of its people. I knew I had to weave that experience into my next novel. It felt like the perfect match for the energy of Water in The Cup—powerful and emotional, with a landscape that echoes Luna and Freya's relationship. It's rough and unforgiving at first, but once they let go of their preconceptions, they connect on a profound level.

The Madigan family dynamics are central across the books—how do you balance supernatural intrigue with relatable familial relationships?

At its core, this story is about family. A lot of the drama stems from their emerging magical talents—which are tightly woven into long-buried family secrets. That connection gives me the perfect opportunity to explore the supernatural while staying grounded in the very real tensions of family life. Honestly, it's one of my favorite things to play with as a writer!

Tarot imagery features beautifully in The Wand—could you elaborate on your collaboration with Nicole Ruijgrok and the role of tarot in storytelling?

It's been such a joy to collaborate with another creative soul! Working with Nicole was incredibly inspiring—she helped bring the visual magic of the cards to life, while also helping me articulate my creative vision in words.

Tarot is deeply interwoven throughout The Madigan Chronicles. Each chapter begins with a Minor Arcana card from one of the suits, setting the tone and subtly foreshadowing the themes ahead. The character traits of the Madigan family are loosely based on the Major Arcana cards they represent in The Magical Tarot Deck, which plays a key role in the second book.

Tarot doesn't just add flavor—it forms the very structure of the story.

Your characters confront both fairy realm politics and modern dilemmas—how do you approach world building to keep both believable and interwoven?

I'm not an overthinker—I love to play and see where the magic leads. One of the beautiful freedoms of writing another realm is the chance to bend reality and gently stretch what readers believe is possible. It allows for a kind of subtle enchantment, expanding horizons without feeling heavy-handed. Fairies may care little for human morals, yet they follow their own intricate and often unyielding code of ethics—and that contrast is endlessly fascinating to explore.

Having Ceri learn as she goes gave me, as the writer, the space to let Fairy grow with her in my imagination. I like to sketch out a path—mapping chapters and story arcs—but I always leave room for discovery. If I plan too tightly, I lose my spark. Creativity needs space to breathe. The subconscious is a powerful guide—trust it.

The Magical Tarot Deck is a captivating sequel in The Madigan Chronicles. Marieke Lexmond weaves a gripping tale of magic, family secrets, and revenge. With imaginative twists, deep emotional exploration, and enchanting illustrations by Nicole Ruijgrok, this book is an immersive journey into modern magical realism that fantasy lovers will adore.

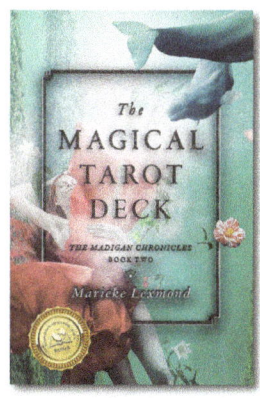

Author Marieke Lexmond, a master of magical realism, invites readers into worlds of wonder and witchcraft with *The Madigan Chronicles*.

The Queen of Fairy ends on a powerful showdown—without spoilers, what themes did you hope readers would resonate with most in that climax?

No spoilers? That's a tough one! But at its heart, I wanted readers to feel the strength that comes from not facing everything alone. There's power in asking for help, and sometimes support arrives from the most unexpected places.

For me, family isn't just about blood—it's about the people who stand by you when it matters most. Whether they're friends, allies, or even brief acquaintances, those connections can be just as vital.

What key piece of advice would you give to aspiring authors hoping to blend magical realism, complex worldbuilding and emotional depth?

Such a great question—because striking that balance isn't easy. The most important thing is to write your first draft without censoring yourself. If you keep editing as you go, you may never finish. Give yourself the freedom to play and let the words flow. That's when the real magic happens—your subconscious might surprise you with little gems you didn't plan.

Once the full story is on the page, then you can start shaping it: balancing worldbuilding with dialogue, emotional depth with structure. And don't be afraid to cut big chunks—nothing is ever wasted. Exploring helps you get to know your characters more intimately, and that depth will shine through.

And one last thing: figure out what works for you. Every writer has a unique process. Courses and outside advice can be incredibly helpful, but in the end, it's about taking what resonates and making it your own. Trust your way!

> *Family isn't just who you're born to—it's the souls who stand beside you as you discover your own magic."*

Marieke Lexmond

An Inspired Journey into Paranormal Thrillers with
SHERRI L. DODD
From Fitness To Fiction Through Grief And Magick

BY DAN PETERS | LONDON

Sherri L. Dodd writes with the soul of a seeker and the heart of a storyteller rooted in wild, myth-laced soil. Raised in the humid, haunted hush of southeast Texas, where ghost stories curl through creek beds and folklore is as natural as bare feet on hot dirt, Dodd learned early that imagination was both sanctuary and compass. Her transition from non-fiction fitness author to the conjurer of Paranormal Thrillers is not a shift—it is a return. With Murder Under Redwood Moon, the first in her Murder, Tea & Crystals trilogy, Dodd steps confidently into the liminal space between reality and the uncanny.

Dodd's fiction is steeped in lived experience—of grief, motherhood, devotion, and mystery. There is a steadying hand behind the wild beauty of her narratives, drawn from years of holistic theology study and spiritual exploration across traditions. Her characters are seekers too, especially Arista, whose journey moves from suspense to transformation across the trilogy's arc. Dodd crafts these tales not merely to entertain, but to illuminate the places where loss sharpens perception, and where belief becomes both a mirror and a map.

What sets her storytelling apart is a quiet, persuasive sense of truth. The magick she writes of is not fantasy for fantasy's sake—it is grounded in natural rhythm, human experience, and spiritual intuition. Whether she's weaving the energies of Sedona's vortexes into her plotlines or recalling a real-life brush with the strange, her work pulses with authenticity.

In a genre too often crowded with noise, Sherri L. Dodd offers resonance. Her stories remind us that mystery doesn't need to shout to be heard—it already lives in the trees, in the desert wind, and in the long shadow of the moon.

Sherri L. Dodd writes with warmth, insight, and originality, crafting layered narratives filled with heart, spirit, and authentic supernatural intrigue.

In Murder Under Redwood Moon, how did your personal experiences with the paranormal influence the story's development?

We lived in the Santa Cruz Mountains for many years, and there is an eeriness to them as well as a comfort. So, my experience with that ambiance brought life to the story. Furthermore, while writing the book, I had a strange encounter which made it into the book—the leopard throw rug incident was taken right out of my own current day life!

What inspired the setting of Sedona, Arizona, in Moonset on Desert Sands, and how does it enhance the narrative?

My husband and I visited Sedona a couple times on the way to hike the Grand Canyon. During the second visit, we walked to a 'male' vortex, but got lost on our way back and ended up running the trail in the darkness with little bats flying at us. That night I had a very unusual anxiety attack about being so far from my children. The metaphysical explanation was that the energy from the vortex disrupted my equilibrium. Pretty powerful effect! So, for book 2 – Moonset on Desert Sands – I thought it would make for an apt setting that Arista and Bethie be part of that new age community.

Sherri L. Dodd shares how her spiritual studies, personal loss, and rich life experience inform her Murder, Tea & Crystals trilogy blending mystery, magick realism, and emotional depth.

In addition, I loved the contrast of the barren desert and red-rocked topography to the lush green redwoods.

Can you discuss the evolution of Arista's character throughout the Murder, Tea & Crystals trilogy?

Read separately, the trilogy starts as a suspenseful, cozy murder mystery in Murder Under Redwood Moon, followed by a psychological thriller in the second book. By the end of book three, I believe the reader will find this trilogy has been Arista's coming of age, comprising her abandonment, trauma, hardships, and finding the ability to rise above the chaos and heartbreak in order to experience her future blessings. The moral being our typical lives can become upended with tragedy, but once trouble passes, we can find meaning and reward are still possible.

How do you balance elements of magick realism with traditional mystery tropes in your writing?

I learned a lot about the modern-day Pagan community while writing this trilogy. I found when you erase the exaggerated theatrics of Hollywood's version of witchcraft, and bring it down to Earth, the balance of magick realism and mystery becomes quite easy. The magick just 'is' … it's a way of looking at the life around us and finding the otherworldly elements in vegetation, animals and events. This is not a supernatural ability; it is something an average person can access, if they have the desire.

Your background includes fitness and motherhood; how have these aspects influenced your storytelling?

My conscientiousness as a mother keeps the sexuality very PG/PG-13 in my books. While my kids are new adults, they don't need to have 'mother's sexuality' shoved in their faces. Not that it's a bad thing, but some things I prefer to keep private. Therefore, what little sex there is in the books could be shown on television. Further, the second book is very mother-oriented—Arista's mother and a secondary pregnant character, and the love and sacrifice those mothers were willing to take for their child. The fitness aspect is translated through the action scenes, whether mountain biking through the redwoods in Murder Under Redwood Moon, the security guard busting into action in book two, or even the physicality of a fight or two in the books. Movement is life!

What challenges did you face transitioning from non-fiction to fiction writing, particularly in the paranormal genre?

Writing about fitness was easy. Learned facts put to paper. Fiction is a vast realm of endless possibilities! Losing my father, I immersed in another world to heal from the loss. For Murder Under Redwood Moon, I kept with the guidance of "is this believable?" Having supernatural experiences, I went with what rang similar. Could it happen? In the final two books of the trilogy, I dug a bit deeper and added more fantasy elements. I'm not talking elves or dragons (which I love), but more to the effect of what you would find

"Murder Under Redwood Moon" brilliantly combines a cozy paranormal vibe with a captivating murder mystery. Sherri L. Dodd's storytelling shines with its rich blend of supernatural elements and suspenseful twists. Arista's journey, full of eerie visions and chilling discoveries, keeps readers enthralled. A must-read for fans of witchy mystical mysteries!

in witchy movies.

How do your personal beliefs and studies in various religions inform the spiritual elements in your novels?

My Bachelor's and, soon-to-be, Master's degrees are in Holistic Theology, and I have studied a few religions. I was raised Episcopalian, confirmed as Catholic in my mid-twenties, spent fourteen years immersed in Buddhism starting in my 30s, and for this trilogy, fell back on my Pagan studies from late teens/early twenties. Rather than focusing on the differences, I see the connections and the possibility for compatibility, especially Celtic Paganism and Catholicism. That is why I made Arista a Celtic Pagan, and her love interest, Shane, a Catholic. There are so many ways that we could drop the fear and, subsequently, anger from our differences and find peace with the similarities.

What advice would you offer aspiring authors interested in blending personal experiences with fictional narratives?

Write what you know. It will come naturally, and people will not have a good basis with which to accuse you of something fake. If you do not know 'it', spend time learning 'it.' Not only will you find enlightenment in your studies, but your story becomes that much more believable.

Author Sherri L. Dodd brings together real-life spirituality and thrilling mystery in her compelling paranormal fiction.

> *We lived in the Santa Cruz Mountains for many years, and there is an eeriness to them as well as a comfort."*

Sherri L. Dodd

Exploring Death, Hope, And Horror Across Realms

Penn Fawn's dark fantasy worlds in Necropolis and The Underworld reimagine the afterlife as a vivid, harrowing continuation where storytelling, philosophy, and visual art converge.

PENN FAWN
CONFRONTS THE AFTERLIFE THROUGH DARK FANTASY AND VISUAL ART

Editor's Desk | London

"What led me to develop it into a series was feedback from a book reviewer who had questions about the background."

Penn Fawn brings readers face-to-face with a shadowy and compelling vision of the afterlife through his dark fantasy series, Necropolis, and its eerie offshoot, The Underworld. Drawing on a rich background in journalism, graphic arts, and digital production, Fawn's career has been interwoven with the printed word in every form. His journey from early fiction experiments stashed away on floppy disks to the publication of acclaimed stories like The Burglar reveals an author who allowed time, experience, and a rekindled creative spirit to shape his voice. What sets Fawn apart is not only the haunting imagination he breathes into his storytelling but the visual dimension he brings through original art, design, and multimedia. With mythic inspiration from sources as disparate as the Bible and Tolkien, his work invites readers to consider the darker terrains of existence, where death does not mean peace, and hope glows dimly in the form of enchanted gems or lone heroes. Through his publishing imprint and artistic ventures, Penn Fawn continues to challenge the borders of genre and media, crafting a uniquely immersive experience in the world of dark fantasy.

What inspired you to create the dark fantasy series, Necropolis, and how did you develop its unique world-building elements?

I wasn't initially thinking about writing a series when I began Necropolis. What led me to develop it into a series was feedback from a book reviewer who had questions about the background and origins of the source material. She mentioned that she hoped I would expand on these elements in future books. I found her points compelling, so I decided to build upon the first book, Necropolis, and that's exactly what I did.

In your spin-off series, The Underworld, you explore a terrifying afterlife. Could you share how you approached blending horror and fantasy in this series?
This might sound like a cliché, but it came very naturally. At no point did blending horror and dark fantasy feel planned, charted, or methodical. The Underworld, as I envisioned it, is a place in the afterlife—a version of hell or purgatory. However, I wanted my Underworld to be more expansive and vividly descriptive than traditional depictions of these realms, such as those in the Bible. While I'm not devout, the Bible—alongside J.R.R. Tolkien's work—was one of my biggest sources of inspiration for this series.

Your short story, "The Burglar," won the Literary Titan Book Award. How did this recognition influence your writing journey?
It didn't influence my journey significantly. Winning awards is great, but the level of prestige determines how much it helps spread the word about your work. While I'm thrilled to have received the Literary Titan Book Award, it's not a widely recognized accolade, so it didn't do much to increase my visibility.

> Fawn masterfully merges horror and fantasy with striking visuals, crafting immersive narratives that explore life beyond death with haunting depth.

As the owner of Darkstar Tees, how do your experiences in graphic arts and clothing design influence the visual aspects of your books?
My background in graphic arts significantly influences the visual elements of my books. Like most authors, I envision the landscapes and creatures in my stories as I write, but sometimes I design these visuals even before finishing the books. If anyone is interested, they can view my artwork on my Pinterest page: Penn Fawn Books.

"Solo" is a short story that delves into the life of a book after its author's death. What inspired you to explore this unique perspective?
The name of the short story is, "The Books," of which Solo is the name of the main character. Although the story is unique—and even comedic—it carries a serious message. It's not just a fun tale about flying books. A bibliophile will likely catch on to its deeper themes quickly. The story is also autobiographical to a degree. I was able to write about the setting in detail because I live in New York, where the story takes place. The Brooklyn Public Library, where Solo finds a home, is a beloved place for me. The story also touches on the tension between traditional and independent publishing.

The Golden Mirage chronicles the journey of men who discover life after death. How do you balance character development with the exploration of philosophical themes in this narrative?
While Lilith, the antagonist, is a central figure, The Golden Mirage also focuses heavily on Hespatia, the "good witch," and her journey. After the many years it took for her to realize her full potential, Hespatia creates the Necropolis within the mountains of Sanctuary, a refuge for men in the Underworld. So, the Necropolis isn't just a burial ground; it's also the name of a magical jewel she crafts to offer hope in the face of seemingly certain or impending doom. The underlying theme is the significance of hope, even in the darkest of times.

Your website mentions a compilation of graphic art meant to introduce readers to your dark fantasy world. How do you see the role of visual art in enhancing the storytelling experience?
Visuals have a more immediate and compelling impact on audiences than the written word. It's no surprise that the film industry reaches broader audiences than books alone. Speaking of visuals, I have a YouTube channel that features music and videos inspired by the settings and characters from Necropolis and The Underworld, including the chief villain, the Necromancer. You can explore them here: Penn Fawn YouTube Channel.

What advice would you offer to aspiring authors looking to blend elements of dark fantasy and horror in their writing?
Study the great works of those who came before you. For me, the Bible is the greatest example of all, but I also recommend devouring everything you can in the genre.

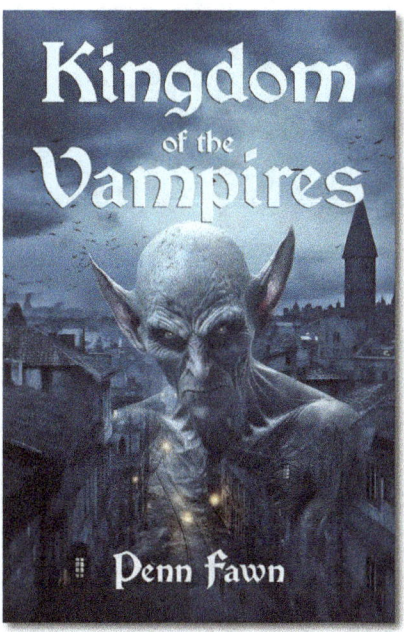

In *Kingdom of the Vampires*, an elderly man named Gib awakens in a strange, eerie realm after death, transformed and bewildered. As he confronts the terrifying reality of a vampire-populated underworld, he questions his beliefs, facing a grim, surreal afterlife in this dark fantasy tale by Penn Fawn.

The Transformative Power of Human-Animal Bonds

Iluta Sutra explores love, healing, and forgiveness in "Saving Gigy," highlighting profound human-animal connections and inspiring readers to self-discovery and empathy.

ILUTA SUTRA
Inspires Through Her Writing on Love, Healing and Forgiveness

"I wrote Saving Gigy as a tribute to the profound bond between humans and animals."

Editor's Desk | London

Iluta Sutra stands as a beacon of inspiration in the literary world, her works embodying a profound exploration of the human spirit and its intricate ties with nature. As an award-winning author, Iluta brings a wealth of cultural richness and soulful depth to her narratives, drawing from her European heritage and diverse life experiences. Her passion for instilling kindness, compassion, love, and forgiveness into the fabric of her stories has not only touched hearts but also resonated deeply with readers across the globe.

At the heart of Iluta's literary journey is her acclaimed work, "Saving Gigy," a poignant tribute to the unique bond between humans and animals. This narrative is woven with threads of empathy and healing, echoing her personal experiences and ardent belief in the transformative power of love and forgiveness. Crafting stories that serve as mirrors for self-discovery, Iluta encourages her readers to reconnect with their true nature, urging them to traverse life's pathways with insight and grace.

Her collaboration with Mariel Hemingway on the book's cover stands as a testament to the thematic integrity and emotional allure of "Saving Gigy." The synergy between Iluta's narrative vision and Hemingway's dedication to animal welfare amplifies the story's impact, inviting readers to embark on an enriching emotional journey. Iluta Sutra's works not only captivate but also inspire, ensuring her position as a cherished luminary in modern literature. Her commitment to crafting narratives that educate, uplift, and inspire is both her mission and her gift to us all.

What inspired you to write "Saving Gigy," and how did your European background influence the narrative?

I wrote "Saving Gigy" as a tribute to the profound bond between humans and animals. Growing up in Europ, I was surrounded by diverse cultures and landscapes that instilled in me a deep appreciation for the beauty of life. This background influenced the narrative by adding a unique blend of cultural richness and emotional depth to the story.

"Saving Gigy" explores profound human-animal connections. How did your personal experiences with pets shape this story?

My personal experiences with pets have been instrumental in shaping the narrative of "Saving Gigy." The love, companionship, and lessons learned from my own pets starting from childhood have been woven into the story, allowing readers to connect with the characters on a deeper level.

The book delves into themes of love, healing, and forgiveness. What message do you hope readers take away regarding these themes?

Through "Saving Gigy," I hope readers take away the message that love, healing, and forgiveness are intertwined and essential for personal growth. The story highlights the transformative power of these themes in overcoming adversity and finding purpose.

Can you share any challenges you faced while writing "Saving Gigy" and how you overcame them ?

One of the main challenges I faced while writing 'Saving Gigy' was crafting the story in a way that conveyed the main message clearly and accurately, while staying true to the facts. I knew how important it was to share this story with the world, and I had to overcome the fear of how it would be received.

How did Mariel Hemingway's involvement in designing the book cover come about, and what impact do you feel it has on readers?

Mariel Hemingway did write a foreword for Saving Gigy. Her passion for animal welfare aligned perfectly with the story's themes. The cover is designed from my vision that suites to the story very well. The cover design has had a significant impact on readers, as it captures the essence of the narrative and invites readers to embark on the emotional journey within.

"Saving Gigy" has received heartfelt reviews from readers. How have these responses influenced your perspective as an author?

The heartfelt reviews from readers have been incredibly touching and have reaffirmed my purpose as an author. Seeing how "Saving Gigy" has resonated with readers and im-

Iluta Sutra writes with profound empathy and insight, weaving heartfelt narratives that inspire readers to embrace love, healing, and deeper connections.

Saving Gigy tells the true story of a beloved cocker spaniel and her devoted owners' mission to find her a loving new home. Highlighting compassion, love, and difficult choices, the book inspires readers to recognise the profound impact of empathy in even the smallest acts of care.

pacted their lives has inspired me to continue creating stories that inspire, educate, and uplift others.

Your website mentions your passion for inspiring others to understand life's true meaning. How does "Saving Gigy" reflect this mission?

"Saving Gigy" reflects my mission by exploring the transformative power of human-animal connections and the lessons they teach us about love, forgiveness, and healing. Through this story, I aim to inspire readers to reevaluate their relationships with animals and the world around them and people.

What advice would you give to aspiring authors seeking to share their unique stories with the world?

To aspiring authors, I would say that the key to sharing your unique story is to stay true to your voice and vision. Be courageous, persistent, and open to growth. Remember that writing is a journey, and the most important thing is to share your message with the world.

Finding Light Through Darkness in Memoir and Crime Fiction

GARY TREW

Shares the Healing Power of Humour and the Weight of Truth

BY DAN PETERS | LONDON

Gary Trew's life and works are nothing short of inspirational. As a British author living in Canada, Gary has seamlessly woven his profound experiences as a child protection social worker, minister, and police officer into narratives that are as raw and insightful as they are darkly humorous. His biography itself reads like a compelling story: a boy who once struggled with bullying, dyslexia, and brain trauma rose above life's adversities to become a celebrated writer, winning literary awards for his gripping memoir *The Hate Game* and the delightfully subversive noir crime novel *An Eye for an Eye: The Mallet Murders*.

Gary's writing is a testament to resilience and transformation. From crafting court reports and briefing notes during his career to producing plays and skits for non-profits and churches, he mastered the power of words long before venturing into published works. Influenced by the absurd brilliance of Monty Python and the poignancy of Joseph Heller, his storytelling effortlessly tempers the darkness with humour, proving that laughter and pain often walk hand in hand.

His memoirs offer more than just a retelling of personal trials; they serve as a lens into wider societal issues, imparting wisdom drawn from decades of public service and personal growth. Whether you're captivated by his reflections on survival or his creative recounting of life's ironies, Gary's stories resonate on multiple levels. His work reminds us that life, no matter how challenging, is an extraordinary tale worth telling.

In this enlightening interview, Gary opens up about the themes that define his journey—from trauma and recovery to the healing power of humour and storytelling. With honesty, wit, and courage, he offers invaluable insights for readers and aspiring writers alike. Prepare to laugh, reflect, and be inspired by a man who has not only endured life's storms but turned them into powerful and relatable stories for us all.

How did your experiences as a child protection social worker, and police officer shape your perspective on resilience and human nature?

In my early working years, Nietzsche's saying, "What doesn't kill you makes you stronger," became my guiding principle as I saw life's pain as something to be embraced and endured. However, it wasn't until I worked in a facility for at-risk youth that I began to view this belief as problematic. I learned that trauma, abuse, and neglect can cause lasting damage to individuals. Past stressors increase the likelihood of developing future mental health issues. Therefore, addressing adverse childhood experiences became crucial for helping children heal and thrive. Through this process, I began to make sense of my own experiences with trauma, which have helped me and others to heal, grow, and develop a healthier outlook on life.

Your memoir details brutal bullying and trauma—was there a particular moment that made you decide to write your story, and was it difficult to revisit those memories?

Gary Trew reflects on trauma, resilience, and the unexpected joys of survival through laughter, writing, and personal transformation in his candid and compelling memoir and fiction.

For many years, I tucked my past experiences away in the back of my mind. As a social worker, I encountered a young person facing similar challenges, which sparked a "Eureka" moment for me: I realised that I had never truly confronted my own trauma. It became apparent that it was time to face my demons, and what better way to do that than by writing a memoir? Revisiting the painful memories of bullying and abuse was difficult because of the guilt and shame I carried. To gain perspective, I reached out to former classmates who validated my experiences and shared their own shocking stories. I knew that this would mean reopening old wounds. I expected to receive praise from some people but also anticipated criticism from others, primarily since some former students viewed their time at Knoll as the best years of their lives.

Humour plays a big role in your writing despite the dark themes—how do you balance the pain and laughter in your storytelling?

Humour has long been my way of coping with stressful situations. At school, students facing bullying often use humour to navigate their harsh experiences and bond with peers. It provided a sense of control in circumstances where we felt powerless. Reporting bullying was futile, as some staff members were even worse than the students, so we would act out in class and share laughter. I remember facing the toughest student in school and laughing afterwards at how surreal it was. While there are moments for seriousness, humour also has its place, and storytellers need to consider their audience, as what amuses one person may not resonate with another.

You mention that meningitis had unexpected effects, like improving your coordination and taste preferences—how do you view these changes now, and have they influenced your approach to life?

Meningitis was both a blessing and a curse. Initially, learning became a massive issue for me. I didn't understand why I suddenly sucked at chemistry and pharmacology at university. Before I got sick, learning was easy for me. After meningitis, I adapted my approach and tapped into my creative side. I colour-coded everything and built 3-D models of atomic structures with Lego pieces. While it took longer to understand concepts, I became a unique "think outside the box" problem solver. When I write my fiction work, I envision a multicoloured movie scene unfolding before my eyes. It's very cool. In an unexpected twist, meningitis has become a remarkable blessing in my life.

You've led a life filled with transformation, from overcoming dyslexia to gaining multiple degrees—what advice would you give to someone facing similar challenges?

I faced many obstacles before returning to university later in life. After being rejected from the UVIC BSW (social work) program, I reapplied the next year with improved grades from supplementary courses. The same

Registrar warned that I might struggle and reluctantly accepted me. I graduated with top marks and an impressive GPA—the Registrar was stunned. Gary, the old man, did it! Therefore, follow your passion, don't give up, and embrace failures and messing up as opportunities for growth.

What was the biggest challenge in writing The Hate Game, and did the process of writing it bring any unexpected personal revelations?

Overcoming guilt and shame was a significant journey for me—I hadn't shared that I had been sexually assaulted, but I felt it was important to include this experience in my narrative. My biggest challenge was battling imposter syndrome, which caused me to doubt my identity and writing abilities. My editor, a creative writing professor, helped me silence the imposter. She said, "If you were one of my students, I would give you a clear distinction. This is some of the best debut writing I've seen."

Your memoir highlights the cruelty of school bullying in the 1970s—do you think things have changed for children today, or do similar patterns still exist in different forms?

The introduction of the National Curriculum, increased parental choices, and improved teacher training have enhanced the education system. At The Knoll, body shaming, homophobia, and physical abuse were prevalent. Nowadays, few schools would tolerate students drawing swastikas on pupils' foreheads or playing playground 'gas chambers,' never mind immersing them in toilet water and urine. Teachers ignored this behaviour—unacceptable today. Reporting misconduct was taboo. However, today's youth are more open about their feelings. While awareness and prevention efforts have reduced bullying, new forms, such as cyber and social bullying, are negatively impacting children.

What advice would you offer to other authors looking to write deeply personal and emotionally challenging memoirs?

I penned this memoir to illuminate my journey of perseverance amid profound adversity, unveiling the unexpected moments of joy I found along the way. It's crucial not to write from a place of anger or revenge. I began to understand generational trauma and the reasons behind family members' behaviours. So, be honest and focus on your personal growth. Reading other memoirs is essential for your journey as a memoir writer. It helps you connect with others, find inspiration, and appreciate the power of personal storytelling. "The Glass Castle" and "Angela's Ashes" inspired me. Westover's "Educated" shares similar yet different experiences, while David Sedaris's "Talk Pretty" memoir is darkly hilarious. Recalling trauma can be difficult, and it's important to understand that hurt people often hurt others. Remember, writing this kind of memoir is not merely about reliving pain and misery—it's about personal transformation, healing and growth.

Gary Trew, award-winning author holds his award-winning book The Hate Game.

Humour has long been my way of coping with stressful situations."

Sherri L. Dodd

Redefining Marginalised Women As Heroes

Susan Rowland discusses her inspiration, Jungian influences, feminist themes, and the challenges of transitioning from academia to crafting rich, thought-provoking mystery novels that champion female resilience and cultural renewal.

SUSAN ROWLAND
Showcases Feminine Heroism And Jungian Depth In Mystery Fiction

Editor's Desk | London

"Mary Wandwalker is so much more than the overlooked feminine, just possibly – a goddess (as we all are)."

Susan Rowland is a luminary in the realm of mystery fiction, seamlessly blending her profound academic insights with her storytelling prowess to create narratives that both intrigue and inspire. With her latest novel, *The Swan Lake Murders*, set to captivate readers from the 1st of June 2025, she delivers yet another masterpiece that delves into the depths of human emotion and the supernatural. Her works are a testament to her brilliance, exploring themes of feminine heroism and cultural renewal through a rich tapestry of Jungian psychology and feminist theory.

In an era where literature seeks to redefine boundaries, Susan Rowland stands as a beacon, championing stories that elevate marginalised women as heroes. Her unique approach to character creation, exemplified by her triple goddess detective, offers readers a refreshing perspective that challenges conventional narratives. *The Swan Lake Murders*, along with her other titles like "Murder on Family Grounds" and "The Alchemy Fire Murder," showcases her ability to weave complex tales that resonate with both intellectual depth and emotional authenticity.

Join us as we delve into a fascinating interview with Susan Rowland, where she shares her inspirations, challenges, and the transformative power of storytelling. Her journey from academia to the captivating world of mystery fiction is not just an exploration of genre, but a quest to unearth the heroism in every enigmatic tale she crafts.

How does Jungian psychology shape the character of Mary Wandwalker in your mystery novels?

Mary Wandwalker is a complex character who has made mistakes, and now quests to find greater meaning. Forced to engage with the world, she discovers her deep intuition and courage enabling her to go beyond everyday experience. Mary balances on the cusp of unconscious marvels. She is so much more than the overlooked feminine, just possibly – a goddess (as we all are). Jung gave me a way of making her real.

What inspired you to create a detective embodying the triple goddess archetype in Murder on Family Grounds?

Robert Graves is credited with popularizing the notion of the triple goddess as maiden, matron and crone. He saw these moon phases as roles for women that would keep them on the margins. What fun to reverse his misogyny! The books see this lunar form of the goddess as models of heroism that can enhance human society through mystery fiction. After all, great writers have given us the older spinster as a formidable detective. And my Anna is not a maiden because she has never had sex. Rather as a survivor of trafficking she grew up without love and is trying to find her way without the moral training of childhood and family. Such survivors are heroes. Finally, my Caroline is motherly, but also suffers from chronic clinical depression. As a hero she reverses the sidelining of mental illness in life

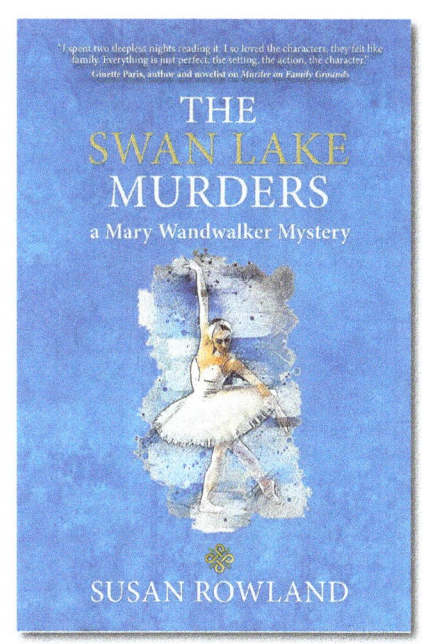

> Susan Rowland is a masterful storyteller whose novels redefine heroism, blending profound intellectual depth and captivating mystery narratives.

and in fiction. Not only is making a good life in such circumstances intrinsically heroic, it also develops undervalued qualities of resilience and empathy.

How do themes of family trauma and patriarchal legacy influence the narrative of Murder on Family Grounds?

In the story we meet three women who have lost, or are about to lose, or have never had, a family. They are Mary Wandwalker who is fired from the nearest thing to a family – her job – after 40 years, Caroline, whose husband loves another woman, and Anna, formerly trafficked and trapped in a crime 'family.' Patriarchy rules in the aristocratic Falconer family that takes primogeniture for granted. But what happens if the son is gay? The compromises forced on gay sons interact with a criminal underworld where patriarchy is dark indeed.

In what ways does The Alchemy Fire Murder explore the element of fire within Jungian symbolism?

Like water in The Sacred Well Murders, earth in Murder on Family Grounds and air in The Swan Lake Murders, fire here stands for a quality innate in humans, and in nature. These elements are archetypal because they are positive for human wellbeing as well as potentially destructive. Fire can be love or rage. It can cook a nutritious meal or burn down a hospital. Where the planet has been terrorized by human greed, fire becomes the climate's revenge and puts relationships and communities at risk, as in this novel set in England and California.

How does your academic background in Jungian studies inform your approach to writing fiction?

I care about Jungian psychology because it places creativity at the heart of being human. It means that living is a quest for meaning both made and found. Novel writing is my quest to receive and translate the energies from the more-than-personal psyche. The novels know more than I do. Writing opens archetypal windows to the cosmos; the characters tell me what they need.

What challenges did you encounter transitioning from scholarly writing to crafting mystery novels?

I expected to find writing fiction difficult. I was not prepared for how endlessly, hugely challenging it is. Scholarly writing has rules, novel writing has demands. The tension between what I might wish to say from my puny conscious ego and what stories stretches me to the limit and more. I wrote three complete drafts before one was close to being publishable.

How do you integrate Jungian Arts-Based Research methodologies into your creative writing process?

JABR means writing from the belief that the unconscious knows more than consciousness and has connections beyond the individual. Therefore we must allow the spontaneity of the psyche to be a full partner in the process.

What role does feminist theory play in reimagining marginalized women as heroes in your novels?

Feminism uncovers and questions the impact of centuries of patriarchy. Any art practice can look again at who is represented and from what partial perspective. By choosing an older woman or crone, a sick woman, and a formerly trafficked woman, I aim to look at the price patriarchy exacts. I make a point of showing that patriarchy also oppresses men.

Crucially, I invoke the cozy mystery in my stories that are far from typical of that genre. For the cozy ends with a positive affirmation of a (usually feminine centered) community. My stories do not depict violence but its consequences. I aim for a comic mode, partly in humor, and in the sense that characters end so much better than they started – and not just the three detectives. My feminism believes in happy endings.

How has your relocation from the UK to the US influenced the settings and themes of your stories?

James Joyce famously said that the way to Ireland was via Holyhead, where he and others departed. Moving to the US probably enabled me to write about 21st century England, although The Alchemy

> Susan Rowland blends Jungian psychology and feminist theory in her mystery fiction to reimagine marginalized women as heroes. Her novels, including *The Swan Lake Murders*, explore trauma, archetypes, and cultural renewal through complex characters. Drawing from academia, she crafts transformative stories that challenge patriarchal norms and celebrate feminine resilience.

Fire Murder, has the murder and much action in California.

What advice would you offer aspiring authors aiming to blend academic insights with creative storytelling?

Do it if you really have to. I have to. I will be writing fiction for the rest of my days. Don't imagine that it will be easy.

NEW YORK TIMES AND USA TODAY BESTSELLING AUTHOR

Insights Into Romance, Trust And Second Chances

JILL SANDERS

The Queen Of Romance, Spinning Timeless Tales That Touch Hearts Across The Globe

as told to Dan Peters

Jill Sanders shares the inspiration behind her bestselling novels, exploring themes of love, trust, resilience, and second chances, while offering heartfelt insights into her creative process and captivating storytelling.

Jill Sanders is a literary force in the world of romance, captivating readers across the globe with her heartfelt stories and unforgettable characters. A New York Times, USA Today, and international bestselling author, Jill has mastered the art of weaving tales that resonate with love, resilience, and the magic of human connection. With over 100 books spanning genres like Sweet Contemporary Romance, Romantic Suspense, Western Romance, and Paranormal Romance, her works have touched countless hearts and earned her a devoted following. Whether it's the charm of small-town life, the thrill of suspense, or the allure of second chances, Jill's stories offer something for every reader, making her a beloved name in the literary world.

Beyond her impressive accolades, Jill's journey as an author is as inspiring as the characters she creates. Raised in the Pacific Northwest and now residing along the Emerald Coast of Florida, Jill draws from her own life experiences to craft vivid settings and relatable themes. Her ability to infuse her novels with warmth, humor, and authenticity has made her a standout voice in the romance genre. In this exclusive interview, Jill shares insights into her creative process, the inspiration behind her beloved characters, and the universal themes that make her stories so impactful. Join us as we delve into the mind of this extraordinary storyteller and celebrate the magic she brings to the page.

Many of your novels draw inspiration from the places you've lived, such as the Pacific Northwest and the Emerald Coast of Florida. How do these locations influence the themes and characters in your stories?

The places I've lived and dreamed of visiting breathe life into my stories. The Pacific Northwest and Emerald Coast of Florida aren't just backdrops; they're characters in their own right, shaping the very soul of my novels. My small hometown, with its tight-knit community, inspired the heart of the Pride Series. There's something magical about a place where everyone knows your name, where you're not just accepted, but embraced. This sense of belonging, of coming home, is what I strive to capture in every story. It's an escape, yes, but also a reflection of the warmth and connection we all crave in our fast-paced world.

Continued *on page 14*

STAR INTERVIEW

" Jill Sanders, The Queen Of Romance, Spinning Timeless Tales That Touch Hearts Across The Globe.

Continued *from page 12*

STAR INTERVIEW

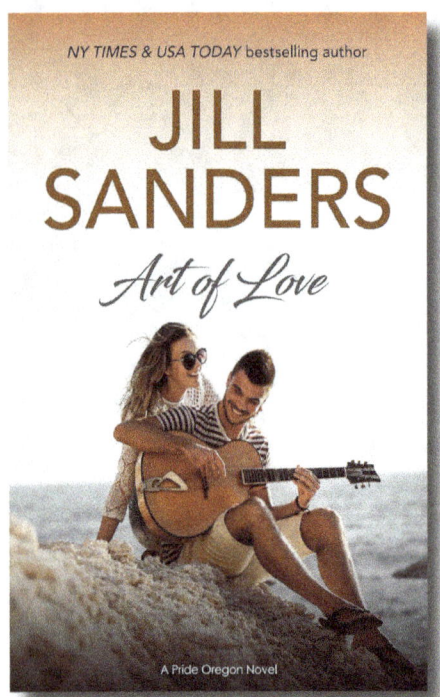

The nineteenth instalment of the Pride Oregon series, Art of Love, delivers Jill Sanders' signature blend of romance and intrigue, set against the picturesque backdrop of her fictional small town. As a standalone entry, the book is accessible even to those unfamiliar with the series while rewarding loyal readers with nods to familiar faces and settings.

The story cleverly weaves together a tale of love, redemption, and suspense as Dylan, a private investigator with a guarded heart, is tasked with uncovering Abe Collins' painful past. Sanders skilfully portrays Dylan's internal conflict between her professional duty and emerging feelings for Abe, a tortured musician who seeks solace in the lighthouse-laden tranquillity of Pride. Their chemistry is both believable and compelling, ensuring readers are invested in their budding relationship.

The novel also explores deeper themes of guilt, fame, and healing, as Abe struggles to reconcile his tragic past with the present. The suspense element, tied to uncovering the truth about a deadly accident, injects an engaging sense of danger that keeps the pages turning.

Sanders' descriptive prose breathes life into Pride's setting, with its coastal charm and intimate community. While certain plot twists feel familiar to avid romance readers, the characters' emotional depth and the high-stakes mystery elevate the story.

Art of Love is a satisfying blend of heartfelt romance and gripping suspense, making it a must-read for fans of small-town dramas and poignant love stories.

With over 90 books across various romance genres, what does your writing process look like? Do you encounter specific challenges when switching between genres like sweet contemporary romance and romantic suspense?

My writing process is a thrilling adventure, sometimes bordering on beautiful chaos! Imagine juggling multiple worlds in your mind – it's exhilarating and challenging. There are days when I have to ground myself firmly in reality to keep all these vibrant characters and rich settings straight. But that's the joy of it! I've developed a system of detailed notes that helps me navigate between genres and stories. It's like having a map to guide me through the vast landscapes of my imagination, ensuring each world remains unique and captivating.

In Finding Pride, Megan Kimble goes through a significant transformation after escaping her past. What was your process for developing her character, and how did you approach her journey toward healing and self-discovery?

Writing Megan's journey in "Finding Pride" was deeply personal and profoundly moving. She's not just a character; she's a tribute to the brave women I've known who've risen from the ashes of their past. Developing Megan was like weaving together threads of courage, resilience, and hope from real-life stories. I wanted readers to feel every step of her transformation, to cheer for her victories and ache for her struggles. It was my way of saying to anyone facing adversity: your happy ending is possible, and your journey matters.

Trust plays a crucial role in Megan's relationship with Todd in Finding Pride, especially after her traumatic experiences. How did you want to portray the themes of trust and redemption in their relationship, and what message do you hope readers take away from their story?

Trust and redemption are the heartbeats of Megan and Todd's story. Drawing from my own 30-year marriage, I wanted to show that true love isn't just about romantic gestures; it's about creating a safe haven for each other's vulnerabilities. Todd isn't just a love interest; he's a mirror reflecting the kind of trust and acceptance we all deserve. Their journey is a testament to the power of love in healing old wounds and building a future on the foundation of mutual respect and unwavering support. It's my hope that readers see in their story the possibility of finding a love that embraces them wholly, flaws and all.

In Last Resort, Cassey and Luke have an undeniable chemistry, despite being on opposite sides of a business deal. How

Jill's journey as an author, inspired by the Pacific Northwest and Florida's Emerald Coast.

Her ability to make settings "characters in their own right."

Insights into her "beautiful chaos" writing process and switching between multiple genres.

STAR INTERVIEW

JILL SANDERS

NY TIMES, USA TODAY BESTSELLING AUTHOR

Jill Sanders is a New York Times, USA Today, and international bestselling author of Sweet Contemporary Romance, Romantic Suspense, Western Romance, and Paranormal Romance novels. With over 100 books in eleven series, translations into several different languages, and audiobooks there's plenty to choose from. Look for Jill's bestselling stories wherever romance books are sold or visit her at jillsanders.com

Jill comes from a large family with six siblings, including an identical twin. She was raised in the Pacific Northwest and later relocated to Colorado for college and a successful IT career before discovering her talent for writing sweet and sexy page-turners. After Colorado, she decided to move south, living in Texas and now making her home along the Emerald Coast of Florida. You will find that the settings of several of her series are inspired by her time spent living in these areas. She has two sons and off-set the testosterone in her house by adopting three furry little ladies that provide her company while she's locked in her writing cave. She enjoys heading to the beach, hiking, swimming, wine-tasting, and pickleball with her husband, and of course writing. If you have read any of her books, you may also notice that there is a love of food, especially sweets! She has been blamed for a few added pounds by her assistant, editor, and fans... donuts or pie anyone?

did you develop their dynamic, and what role does conflict play in shaping their relationship throughout the story?

Cassey and Luke's story in "Last Resort" was a joy to write! Their chemistry sizzles with the tension of being on opposite sides, yet drawn together by an irresistible force. Cassey, with her fiery spirit and the blessing of a loving adopted family, collides wonderfully with Luke's world of wealth and family complications. Their conflict isn't just a plot device; it's the crucible that forges their connection, challenging them to see beyond their differences. It's like watching two puzzle pieces that seem mismatched at first, slowly revealing how perfectly they fit together.

The story revolves around themes of resilience and second chances. What inspired you to explore these themes in Last Resort, and how do you think they resonate with readers in today's world?

Second chances and resilience are themes that resonate deeply with all of us, especially in today's world. Who hasn't wished for a do-over or faced seemingly insurmountable obstacles? In "Last Resort," I wanted to explore the beautiful truth that our past doesn't define us; it's how we rise from our challenges that shapes our future. These themes are universal and timeless, offering hope and inspiration. They remind us that every setback is an opportunity for a comeback, and that with courage and perseverance, we can rewrite our own stories. It's about finding strength we didn't know we had and daring to dream of better tomorrows●

Jill Sanders is a visionary author whose heartfelt romances inspire readers with their authenticity, passion and universal themes of love.

Navigating Mystical Traditions

Alman D Guide shares insights on spiritual traditions, blending analytical thinking with mystical wisdom, guiding readers on a transformative journey.

ALMAN D GUIDE
EXPLORES THE MYSTICAL PATH TO SPIRITUAL ENLIGHTENMENT

Editor's Desk I London

"The Fool's Path is a metaphor for the modern spiritual seeker's journey toward self-realization."

Alman D Guide, a name synonymous with spiritual exploration and profound insight, graces the pages of our upcoming issue with an interview that promises to enlighten and inspire. Known for his unique ability to blend analytical thinking with spiritual wisdom, Alman D Guide, or Alfredo J. Parra, has carved a niche in the literary world that transcends conventional boundaries. His works, "The Fool's Path: A Glance at The Spiritual World" and "El Camino del Loco: Una Mirada al mundo espiritual," are not just books but gateways to a deeper understanding of the mystical traditions that shape our world.

As an author, Alman D Guide invites readers to embark on a journey of self-discovery, encouraging them to become co-creators of their destiny. His writings are a testament to his ability to distill complex spiritual concepts into accessible wisdom, making them essential reading for anyone seeking to navigate the intricate landscape of spirituality. Through his teachings, he offers a harmonious blend of the analytical and the intuitive, the practical and the mystical, providing a roadmap for living with purpose and meaning in today's complex world.

In this interview, Alman D Guide shares his journey, insights, and the challenges he has faced in presenting diverse spiritual beliefs with respect and authenticity. His dedication to honouring traditional practices while making them relevant to modern readers is evident in every word. As you delve into this conversation, prepare to be captivated by the depth of his knowledge and the warmth of his guidance.

Alman D Guide introduces a unique hypothesis: a direct relationship between Tarot and the Simulated Universe or Matrix. He views Tarot as a tool to navigate and understand our position within the Matrix, offering profound insights into our spiritual journey.

In "The Fool's Path," you delve into various spiritual traditions; how did you select which traditions to include?

It was guided by three key principles: universality, symbolic resonance, and transformative potential. These were chosen not to represent a comprehensive overview of world religions, but to highlight archetypal themes that resonate across cultures, such as the hero's journey, surrender, inner awakening, and integration of opposites. Traditions like Zen Buddhism, Sufism, Hermeticism, Christian mysticism, indigenous shamanism, and Kabbalah were included because they each offer unique yet complementary insights into the soul's journey through unknowing, initiation, ego dissolution, and ultimate unity. The Fool, as a seeker archetype, naturally crosses boundaries and borrows wisdom wherever it can be found, so the path is intentionally eclectic, mirroring the lived experience of many modern seekers.

"El Camino del Loco" explores esoteric concepts; what inspired you to write this book in Spanish?

Although I was born in New York, during my childhood family relocated in South America. Writing in Spanish reflects my desire to connect more deeply with Spanish-speaking readers, making the ideas more accessible and resonant. I also have a personal and cultural tie to the Spanish-speaking world, which influenced my choice. Finally,

> Alman D Guide masterfully bridges the gap between analytical thought and spiritual insight, offering profound wisdom and transformative guidance.

publishing in Spanish opens the door to a broader audience of readers interested in following a spiritual path. All these factors made me decide to reach readers in a language that enhances both meaning and impact.

Both your books discuss mystical practices; how do you ensure accessibility for readers new to these topics?

I wanted to ensure that my mystical works remain accessible to new readers by blending deep spiritual insights with a clear, conversational tone. I use storytelling, symbolism, and thoughtful questions to guide readers gently into complex ideas, avoiding technical jargon and instead focusing on relatable themes like personal growth, transformation, and inner freedom. By grounding ancient wisdom in modern life and encouraging exploration over doctrine, I create a welcoming path for those beginning their spiritual journey.

Your works feature tarot symbolism; how do you interpret the Fool's journey in a modern context?

I interpret it as a metaphor for the modern spiritual seeker's path toward self-realization. The Fool isn't portrayed as naive or careless, but as courageous: someone willing to step into the unknown, question conventional beliefs, and trust the unfolding of inner wisdom. In a modern context, I frame this journey not as escapism, but as an act of conscious rebellion against societal conditioning and surface-level living. The Fool becomes a symbol of authenticity, encouraging readers to shed roles, embrace vulnerability, and reconnect with their intuition. This path involves risk, doubt, and solitude, but also wonder, freedom, and transformation. Rather than seeing spiritual awakening as a distant or abstract ideal, I present it as a deeply personal, ongoing process accessible to anyone willing to take that first step, even if they don't have all the answers.

As a researcher of spiritual traditions, what challenges have you faced in presenting diverse beliefs respectfully?

I faced several key challenges. One key challenge was balancing the need to honor traditional practices and philosophies while making them relevant to modern readers. Spiritual traditions are deeply rooted in culture and history, and I had to ensure I represented these beliefs accurately without oversimplifying or distorting them, another challenge was navigating cultural sensitivity, as spiritual practices often come with distinct values and customs. I needed to avoid cultural appropriation and instead approach each tradition with genuine respect and understanding. Additionally, I had to tread carefully to avoid presenting any one spiritual path as superior, emphasizing the personal nature of spiritual journeys rather than pushing a singular ideology. Also, I had to handle the integration of complex mystical symbols like those found in Tarot, Kabbalah, and alchemy in a way that was accessible to a diverse audience. This meant making the rich, layered meanings of these symbols clear without alienating those unfamiliar with the traditions from which they originated. Finally, in a world where spirituality is increasingly inclusive, I had to ensure my work spoke to readers of various backgrounds, offering wisdom that could complement rather than challenge their personal beliefs.

How has reader feedback influenced your approach to writing about the spiritual world?

I believe reader feedback had a significant influence on my approach to writing about the spiritual world. As with any author exploring complex and deeply personal subjects, responses from readers had offered valuable insights into how my work was being received and whether it resonated effectively. For example, if readers found certain concepts too difficult to grasp, I refined my language or provided more practical examples to make the material more accessible. Likewise, feedback from a diverse audience encouraged me to ensure my work was inclusive and could speak to readers from various spiritual backgrounds, prompting me to explore universal themes rather than adhering too strictly to any one tradition. Moreover, stories of personal transformation shared by readers inspired me to incorporate more relatable, narrative-driven elements into my writing, showing how spiritual practices manifest in everyday life.

What role does personal experience play in your exploration of esoteric subjects?

Personal experience played a central role in my exploration of esoteric subjects. Rather than approaching spirituality as a detached academic topic, my writing is rooted in lived experience, reflection, and inner transformation. This makes my material not only more authentic but also

> *The Fool's Path* by Alman D Guide is an accessible, inspiring guide to spiritual growth, blending personal stories with esoteric wisdom. Covering Tarot, universal laws, and mystical tools, it challenges perceptions of reality while offering practical advice. A thought-provoking read for both beginners and seasoned spiritual seekers.

more relatable for readers on their own spiritual paths. In El Camino del Loco and The Fool's Path, personal experience serves as both the entry point and the guiding thread. I often used introspective observations, emotional honesty, and symbolic journeys to illustrate how spiritual truths unfold not just through study, but through direct engagement with life through doubt, solitude, insight, and inner struggle. Esoteric knowledge is not presented as a set of abstract ideas to be memorized, but as a process to be felt, questioned, and lived.

What advice would you offer aspiring authors interested in writing about spirituality and mysticism?

My advice to aspiring authors who feel called to write about spirituality and mysticism begins with a deep commitment to personal truth and lived experience. Spiritual writing is not about presenting lofty theories or polished answers, it's about sharing the raw, evolving journey of the soul in a way that others can feel and relate to. The most resonant works in this genre come from a place of inner work and reflection, where the writer has not only studied mystical ideas but allowed them to transform their life. Writing from that place of authenticity builds trust with the reader and offers something far more valuable than abstract knowledge: real, human insight into the spiritual path.

Exploring the Detective Emilia Cruz Series

Carmen Amato discusses her journey from CIA to crime fiction, her inspirations, and the strong female protagonists in her award-winning novels.

CARMEN AMATO
Weaves Intrigue and Authenticity into Crime Fiction

by Dan Peters | London

"Detective Emilia Cruz would be up against cartels, corruption and machismo as the first female police detective in Acapulco."

Carmen Amato is a masterful storyteller whose works have captivated readers with their intricate plots and compelling characters. Her Detective Emilia Cruz series, set against the vibrant yet perilous backdrop of Acapulco, offers a thrilling exploration of crime, corruption, and social inequality. Amato's unique perspective, honed from a distinguished career with the CIA, infuses her narratives with authenticity and depth, making each novel a gripping read.

Her accolades, including the prestigious Silver Falchion Award for "Murder at the Galliano Club," underscore her talent for weaving historical intrigue with personal tales of resilience and courage. Amato's ability to draw from real-life experiences and historical events enriches her storytelling, providing readers with a vivid and immersive experience.

In this issue of Reader's House magazine, we delve into the mind of Carmen Amato, exploring the inspirations behind her acclaimed series and standalone thrillers. Her insights into the craft of writing and her dedication to portraying strong female protagonists offer invaluable lessons for aspiring authors. Join us as we celebrate the remarkable achievements of Carmen Amato, a true luminary in the world of crime fiction.

How did your CIA experience influence Emilia Cruz's character and the depiction of Acapulco's criminal underworld?

After a career focus on technical collection and counterdrug efforts, I knew that Detective Emilia Cruz would be up against cartels, corruption and machismo as the first female police detective in Acapulco.

Gorgeous beaches and towering skyscrapers line the most beautiful bay in the world. But there is appalling poverty in neighborhoods far from the water.

Ground zero for the war on drugs, Acapulco has one of the highest homicide rates in the Western Hemisphere.

This tension between high and low continually challenges Emilia to choose between police work and personal life.

In Barracuda Bay, Emilia becomes a fugitive in Washington, D.C.; what inspired this shift from Acapulco?

Barracuda Bay is the 9th book in the series. It was time to send her out of her comfort zone.

In the US, Emilia faces the worst situation imaginable. Witness to a murder, she barely escaped with her life and is now on the run in a strange country. Killers disguised as cops are hunting her.

It's November. She has no coat, cell phone, money, car, passport or refuge.

How is she going to survive?

> Carmen Amato crafts thrilling narratives with authenticity, drawing from her CIA experience to create unforgettable crime fiction.

Narco Noir was inspired by a real crime involving a taxi driver; how do real events influence your storytelling?

I keep a file with stories about crime in Mexico and Central America that provide inspiration for the Detective Emilia Cruz series.

Narco Noir was inspired by the murder of a taxi driver in Honduras. A gang was extorting drivers. When the drivers finally filed a police report, the gang retaliated by shooting the first driver in line.

Of course, Emilia goes undercover as a taxi driver to catch the killer.

The Hidden Light of Mexico City delves into political corruption; what motivated you to explore this theme?

Having spent several years in Mexico, I wanted to write about the country's rigid class system. Adding current events to make a political thriller proved to be a winning formula. The book was Longlisted for the 2020 Millennium Book Prize.

In the book, the Secretary of Public Security colludes with an El Chapo-like druglord to buy Mexico's presidency. An attorney discovers the collusion even as he becomes involved with a woman from the opposite end of the social spectrum, in a Cinderella-story subplot.

I felt like a psychic a few years after The Hidden Light of Mexico City was published, when Genaro García Luna, the former Secretary of Public Security was found guilty of accepting millions from the Sinaloa cartel.

The Galliano Club series is based on your grandfather's tales; how did his stories shape the narrative?

My grandfather was a deputy sheriff of Oneida County in the 1920s during Prohibition who told us stories of his escapades that became the foundation for the books.

For example, one night he was sent to a cemetery. Bootleggers had held a funeral complete with a casket thought to be full of illegal booze. My grandfather was supposed to arrest them when they came back to dig it up.

He didn't want to go alone so he asked his best friend, an insurance salesman, to go along.

It was a cold and blustery night. The night sky over the cemetery was pitch black as they huddled behind a headstone. They waited . . .

Ten or fifteen minutes. If the bootleggers came back for their booze, they were welcome to it!

Murder at the Galliano Club won the 2023 Silver Falchion Award; what elements do you believe contributed to its success?

The book delivers the unexpected. It's an American 1920s Prohibition tale but not a frothy flapper or Chicago gunsel story. The setting is an industrial town. Immigrants work in the copper mills and want a beer when the whistle blows.

Murder at the Galliano Club centers on the rivalry between Luca Lombardo, a recent immigrant who runs a social hub for Italian men and Benny Rotolo, an ambitious bootlegger who hates Al Capone.

Every character has a secret, including the vaudeville dancer who lives above the club and witnesses the murder that could destroy everyone connected to the Galliano Club.

Your novels often feature strong female protagonists; what drives your focus on women's experiences in crime fiction?

I joined the Central Intelligence Agency at a time when women were just beginning to rise into positions of greater responsibility. Many times, I was the only woman in the room.

Some of my experiences are in the Detective Emilia Cruz series, such as when a male colleague said he never worked with a woman before and will make Emilia's life miserable until she quits.

As with me, this wasn't exactly news to Emilia!

My female friends are strong women who rose to significant leadership positions at the CIA. My mother and maternal grandmother were both strong women who met life challenges with grit and grace.

Write what you know, as the saying goes.

What advice would you offer aspiring authors aiming to write compelling crime and thriller novels?

First, find role models, read their books and identify what makes them compelling.

Second, learn to outline. Complex plots rarely happen by accident.

Third, don't fall in love with your first draft. The first draft is just shoveling sand into the sandbox so you can make a castle later.

Russian Mojito follows Detective Emilia Cruz as she recovers from a cartel ambush, only to face her stepfather's kidnapping and a Russian guest's murder. Amid rising danger, Emilia uncovers ties between fuel theft and Russian crime, leading to a deadly showdown. A gripping, internationally charged police procedural thriller.

A Journey Through Creativity, Romance, and Historical Truths

Stephanie Cowell discusses the inspirations behind her acclaimed novels, her transition from opera to writing, and how music, history, and vision shape her characters, settings, and emotional storytelling.

STEPHANIE COWELL
Blends Art, Music and Imagination into Timeless Historical Fiction

Editor's Desk | London

I have a very lyrical writing style, quite cadenced. And I think of the novel in sections like chamber music."

Stephanie Cowell is an extraordinary literary voice, a true connoisseur of history, passion, and artistry. Her ability to transport readers into evocative worlds filled with the struggles and triumphs of creative souls is nothing short of remarkable. From her lyrical writing style, undoubtedly influenced by her background in classical singing, to her vivid portrayal of historical figures like Claude Monet, Shakespeare, and Mozart, Cowell crafts narratives brimming with depth, emotion, and humanity. As a recipient of the American Book Award, her mastery of storytelling continues to earn admiration from readers across the globe.

With novels such as *Claude & Camille: a novel of Monet*, *Marrying Mozart*, *The Players: a novel of the young Shakespeare*, and the poignant *The Boy in the Rain*, Stephanie Cowell captures moments in history with tenderness and an unparalleled sense of authenticity. Her forthcoming novel, *The Man in the Stone Cottage*, promises a fresh and enthralling perspective on the Brontë sisters' lives, blending historical reality with the mystique of the imagination.

Through her stories, Cowell reminds us why the arts and our connection to the past remain vital to the human spirit. It is a privilege to delve into the mind of a creator who continually bridges history and heart, inspiring readers with tales of love, resilience, and creative endeavor.

In "The Boy in the Rain," you explore a same-sex relationship in Edwardian England. What inspired

you to delve into this period and subject matter?

In the mystical way my stories often happen to me, I had a vision while walking down the outer wooden stair by a country house of two men standing there in circa 1900 clothes. When I turned around, they were gone but they kept haunting me. I finally told two friends who challenged me to write something of them down. I did but it was horribly rough. I was an opera singer then, not a writer. I left music and began to write novels but "The Boy in the Rain" always seemed to want another draft and my then major publishers felt an Edwardian love story of two guys would not sell enough copies. After I had published five other novels, a friend sent me to a small publisher who loved it. From first notes to first printed copy, it had been a journey of 39 years.

Your novel "Claude & Camille" portrays Claude Monet's early life and love. How did you balance historical accuracy with creative storytelling?

I grew up the daughter of artists and was taken to art galleries since I can remember. Over and over, I heard the stories of the struggles of great artists. One day I when my writing career was well launched, I went to an exhibition of the early impressionists at a museum and there was a small, intimate

> Cowell is a masterful storyteller whose lyrical prose and deep historical insight breathe life into the forgotten corners of art and history.

painting done by the artist Bazille of all his friends (including Monet, Renoir etc.) in his studio in Paris circa 1869 when they were unknown. I was so struck by the fierce friendship between them and the determination they would all succeed. For research, I think I bought and read about 75 books and visited many museums. But the day-to-day life you have to create as we don't know exact conversations. So you respectfully create based on history. I had an awful time with finding much about Camille, Monet's muse, model and wife. During my writing of the novel, someone found a diary speaking of her written in Paris 1860s. It was discovered in a box in a closet no one had cleaned out in over 150 years.

"Marrying Mozart" focuses on the Weber sisters and their relationships with Mozart. What drew you to their lesser-known stories?

I sang a great deal of Mozart opera over many years, and always thought I'd write about him. I was sitting in a Viennese café one day as a cd played one of his horn concertos which was so utterly happy, and I remembered years before reading that he had had been close friends with the four musical daughters of a second violinist at the court orchestra in Mannheim. And that he had been 21 and lonely and looking for jobs, and one girl had jilted him, but he eventually married another. I wrote the plot a little like a Mozart opera. It is my happiest book.

In "The Players," you depict Shakespeare's formative years. What challenges did you face in bringing such an iconic figure to life?

I truly had to use imagination for that because very little is known about his early years. I have loved the plays since I was very young, and I read an amazing number of scholars. The great Elizabethan scholar A.L. Rowse told me to study the sonnets which became the heart of the book. I still have my tiny blue sonnet book, quite marked and tattered.

Your upcoming novel, "The Man in the Stone Cottage," explores the Brontë sisters' struggles. What new perspectives do you aim to offer on their lives?

I had spent days in the Brontë parsonage in Haworth, Yorkshire, which remains much as it was in the 1840s when the book takes place. It is very haunted. I felt the three sisters and the brother in such an intense way. The book is secondly about the bonds between sisters and the search for love and the struggle to keep the roof over their heads. They were poor. But the main story is a man Emily discovers in a stone cottage on the moor and becomes intensely close to though no one else has ever seen him. Is he real? And what is reality? How much do all of us create in some ways those we love? And do they then walk the earth?

Many of your works centre on artists and musicians. What fascinates you about creative figures from history?

I grew up in a family and a community of artists. It never occurred to me to find a profession in anything else but the arts. All other work was somehow not quite real to me.

How has your background in classical singing influenced your approach to writing historical fiction?

I have a very lyrical writing style, quite cadenced. And I think of the novel in sections like chamber music or opera. Parts are allegro, quick and sprightly.

What advice would you give to aspiring authors interested in writing historical novels?

I think you need to fall entirely in love with a period of history andwant to know it in its smallest detail. The challenging thing is making the reader see enough detail to

The Fool's Path by Alman D Guide is an accessible, inspiring guide to spiritual growth, blending personal stories with esoteric wisdom. Covering Tarot, universal laws, and mystical tools, it challenges perceptions of reality while offering practical advice. A thought-provoking read for both beginners and seasoned spiritual seekers.

know we are in a very different time, but all through a character's eyes. The characters have to be as real as people crowding you in a bus. It's wonderful that they know things that you do not and do things differently yet feel so much of what you feel.

Exploring Love, Identity, and Self-Acceptance Through Character-Driven Stories and Humour

Daryl Banner discusses his bestselling Spruce Texas series, the emotional depth behind his characters, the balance of humour and heartbreak, and why writing romance is both a passion and a purpose.

DARYL BANNER

Shares How Music, Psychology, and Small-Town Stories Shape His Unforgettable Gay Romance Novels

Editor's Desk | London

"Bridger just can't hold back from criticizing Anthony's recklessness, and Anthony can't help but 'poke the bear' of Bridger's stoicism."

Daryl Banner brings a bold blend of heartfelt emotion, wit, and musicality to the pages of his beloved romance novels. A USA Today Bestselling author with a background in theatre and psychology, he infuses his stories with both narrative depth and dramatic flair. His Spruce Texas Romance series—beginning with Football Sundae—has blossomed into a fan-favourite collection exploring love, identity, and self-acceptance in a small-town setting. With dynamic characters who tug at readers' hearts and dialogue as rhythmic as a melody, Banner captures the complexity of human connection with both humour and vulnerability. Whether writing opposites-attract love stories or crafting sweeping, time-spanning sagas like When I See You Again, he invites readers to witness characters breaking free of their emotional armour to discover something real. In this exclusive interview, Banner reflects on his creative journey, the psychology behind his characters, and why writing romance has become more than a calling—it's a mission.

What first inspired you to write the Spruce Texas Romance series, and did you always envision it becoming a long-running series?

I wanted to reinvent my own experiences growing up gay in Texas, which is how I came about writing Football Sundae, the first book in the Spruce Texas series. It was intended as just a stand-alone romance, but after receiving so much love from readers, I realized there were many more stories to tell in Spruce. I just released the 9th book "Hot Mess Express" with a 10th in development and am still having so much fun writing them, which I suppose is a good sign!

"Hot Mess Express" features a strong contrast between Bridger and Anthony—how did you balance the tension and humour in their relationship?

Honestly? I didn't. I let them go way off balance whenever it pleased them. Bridger is uptight and controlling, recently discharged from the Army. Anthony is wild and unapologetic. At moments it felt like the scenes were writing themselves. Bridger just can't hold back from criticizing Anthony's recklessness, and Anthony can't help but "poke the bear" of Bridger's stoicism. I loved letting these guys "take the lead" in directing the plot, more or less, having faith they'll find their own balance once they open up to each other. And boy, do they ever.

How do you go about developing such dynamic chemistry between your characters, particularly in opposites-attract scenarios?

One of the most profound things I learned pursuing my degree in psychology was the myth of "opposites attract", which still to this day affects my writing. We build walls and defenses through our lives to protect ourselves from being hurt, and underneath, there's a vulnerable part that never changes, like our inner child. That's where alleged opposites find their common ground. I have so much fun playing with the idea of what people seem like versus who they really are inside. It's

> Daryl Banner masterfully blends wit, warmth, and vulnerability, crafting emotionally rich romances that resonate deeply with readers around the world.

like a smirking promise of what's to come when these "seeming opposites" collide.

Your books often explore themes of identity and self-acceptance. How important is it for you to represent these journeys in small-town settings?

Readers regularly comment wishing Spruce, Texas actually existed, because they love "living there" in the pages and feel the town and my characters give them hope. I was brought to tears from an email I got recently where a gay man said that through my books, he "experienced the love life he always wanted" and felt he'd missed out on. It makes me feel like my being an author is less of a career and more of a mission.

Do you have a favourite character from the Spruce Texas or Texas Beach Town series, and if so, what makes them special to you?

I'm so afraid to pick a favorite and have all the rest glare at me. But I choose Noah from "Mr. Picture Perfect". He lives inside his head, which is me in a nutshell. Many readers reacted positively to Noah, noting he seems neurodivergent and seeing themselves in how he navigates the world. The love interest Cole is a "perfect" (pun intended) complement to Noah.

How do your skills as a composer influence your storytelling? Do you find similarities between writing music and writing fiction?

When I compose, I always keep a story in my head. I've been composing since I was a kid and was mostly inspired by video game music growing up, which might explain why I've always experienced music as a story. I never skip tracks when I listen to an album because I feel like it's the same as skipping chapters in a book.

What's your process like when starting a new book—do you plot thoroughly or let the characters lead the way?

Usually, my books start with a single idea: a character, situation, or concept. Then I think about it—a lot. It's important for the story to develop organically and not be contrived, which is something my time as a theatre/playwrighting major in college taught me. Outlining can be useful if your story has many moving parts (like my dystopian and fantasy series). But I still need to leave space for the characters to "play". My favorite thing is surprising myself: "Oh, they want to do this now? Okay, let's see what happens." Isn't that how life is sometimes?

"When I See You Again", an Amazon Celebrity Pick of 2021, touches on family dynamics and personal responsibility. How do you weave deeper emotional themes into a romantic plot?

"When I See You Again" is one of my favorite stories I've written, and that's due to its deeper themes and unique storytelling structure, with every chapter taking place 5 years later. I sat on the idea for many years, unsure how to tell the story of Caleb and Beau, and scrapped my first chapter probably four times before finally finding the "voice" of the book. I set out to showcase how love can grow in unlikely places over the course of an entire lifetime as well as how that love can change—from curiosities felt as children, to the turmoil of teenage crushes, to juggling the burdens of young adult life and beyond. The story continues beyond the happily-ever-after. My challenge as an author was writing complex, sometimes painful scenes while also preserving the humor, heart, and excitement of falling in love. Stories can amuse and arouse you with the same amount of intensity as they can devastate.

What advice would you give to aspiring authors hoping to build engaging, heartfelt romance series that resonate with readers?

As cliché as it sounds: stay true to yourself. From my own experience, I can say you won't remember the release of any specific book. You won't remember that one awful thing that one person said. Or the crick in your neck from hunching over the keyboard for hours. What you'll remember is the indescribable glory of

> *Hot Mess Express* follows Bridger, a stoic Army vet seeking peace in Spruce, Texas, who clashes with Anthony, a chaotic party boy. Their fiery enemies-to-lovers journey unfolds with humour, heart, and heat, as tension turns to unexpected romance in this steamy, small-town M/M love story full of personality.

writing that unexpected dramatic scene. You'll remember the passion in your heart when a new brilliant idea occurred to you mid-chapter. You'll remember when you were brave enough to "go there" and choose the risky option for your story, challenging yourself. You'll remember the pain of realizing a character must die despite your efforts to save them. It's the "moments" that will mean the most to you as an artist. Stay true to yourself and to the stories you wish to tell, no matter how strange they seem or how far they stray from what others are reading right now. If you can forgive me for being an overdramatic poetic mess: That unwritten story living in your heart right now is your prisoner, and you are (literally) the only person on the entire planet who can free it. The key is to make solid choices, risk making mistakes along the way, and just write. It is absolutely your responsibility to free that story. You're the hero of your inspiration. Rescue it, care for it, and set it aflight.

EDITOR'S CHOICE

NOVEL • STORY • LITERATURE

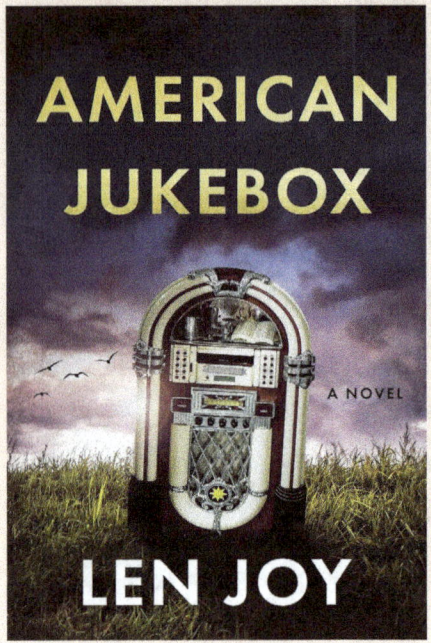

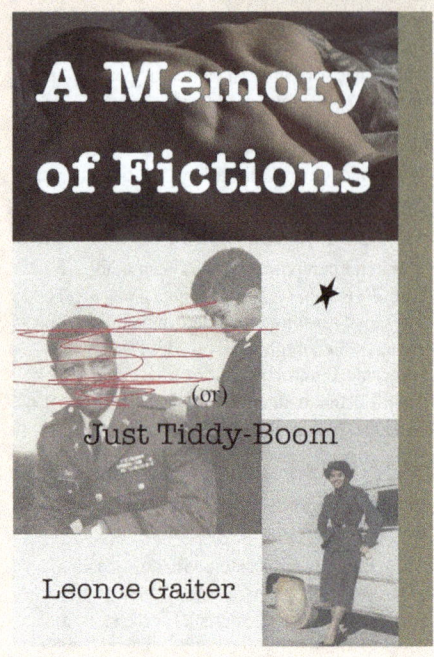

AMERICAN JUKEBOX
by Len Joy

A MEMORY OF FICTIONS
by Leonce Gaiter

LIT
by Mark Anthony

A beautifully written, character-driven story that masterfully explores family, identity, and resilience with heartfelt emotion and relatable depth.

A daring, lyrical masterpiece—Gaiter's voice is unforgettable, weaving raw honesty and poetic brilliance into a fiercely original narrative.

LIT is an exceptional blend of suspense, originality, and emotional depth, delivering a thrilling and unforgettable reading experience.

Len Joy's *American Jukebox* is an evocative and heartfelt exploration of the intricacies of family, identity, and small-town life in late 20th century America. Through the lens of Clayton Stonemason's struggles, the novel deftly captures the duality of admiration and disappointment inherent in familial bonds, particularly the idolisation of a flawed father figure.

Joy's storytelling is poignant and layered, providing readers with a vivid glimpse into Clayton's emotional journey as he attempts to escape the shadows of his father's downfall. The novel thrives on its authentic portrayal of small-town dynamics, intertwining themes of legacy, aspiration, and personal redemption. The setting feels tangible and lived-in, and the characters, particularly Clayton, are crafted with a level of depth that makes them truly resonate.

One of the book's most compelling qualities is its ability to balance moments of introspection with broader reflections on societal change. Joy paints a relatable picture of a young man wrestling with his place in the world, creating a growth arc that feels both realistic and inspiring.

While the narrative flows smoothly for the most part, there are points where the pacing falters slightly as the story delves extensively into its themes. Nevertheless, the depth of insight and the emotional resonance more than compensate for these minor lapses.

American Jukebox is a well-crafted tale that will appeal to fans of coming-of-age narratives and readers who relish character-driven stories. Highly recommended for those seeking a poignant and thought-provoking read.

Leonce Gaiter's *A Memory of Fictions (or) Just Tiddy-Boom* is a bold and jazz-infused literary journey through memory, identity, and survival. At once experimental and deeply grounded in emotional truth, the novel defies convention in both form and theme, weaving memoir, poetry, images, and prose into a powerful coming-of-age narrative.

At its core is Jessie Vincent Grandier, a gay, Black man born to a socially stratified Creole mother and a rough-hewn military father. Spanning from the late 1950s through the Reagan era, the book charts Jessie's painful and defiant quest to reconcile the clashing worlds of his upbringing with the complexities of his own identity. Whether navigating Harvard's elite halls or LA's smoky gay bars, Jessie remains both acutely aware of, and at odds with, the societal and familial expectations forced upon him.

Gaiter's prose is muscular, musical, and unapologetically raw. His style swings between brutal candour and poetic introspection, often within the same page. There's a defiant brilliance in how he captures dislocation—racial, sexual, and emotional—through Jessie's perspective, without ever slipping into self-pity. The novel is not merely a story of one man, but a deconstruction of the American Black bourgeois family and its generational burdens.

Unflinching yet tender, disjointed yet cohesive, *A Memory of Fictions* is a post-modern triumph. Gaiter has crafted something wholly original—achingly personal, culturally rich, and resonant with universal questions of truth, belonging, and redemption.

Mark Anthony's *LIT* is an engaging and darkly atmospheric start to *The Lit Series*, immediately drawing readers into a world where anguish and terror collide. The story offers a fresh take on supernatural horror, centring on Leviathans—malevolent entities that prey on damaged souls, turning their inner turmoil into an endless feast of suffering. The author's depiction of these creatures is both unsettling and fascinating, creating a tense backdrop that grips the reader from the outset.

At the heart of the tale are three Conduits, individuals marked by their pain and targeted by the relentless Leviathans. Their plight is tragic yet strangely relatable, and Anthony does a commendable job of capturing the raw vulnerability of their existence. The tension builds masterfully with the approach of the Circle—a potentially life-altering event that raises the stakes and deepens the mystery. Amidst the horror, themes of friendship and trust are beautifully woven in, offering glimmers of hope in an otherwise oppressive narrative.

Anthony's prose is vivid, balancing poetic descriptions with pulse-pounding sequences. While the pacing occasionally slows during introspective moments, this serves to enhance the emotional depth of the characters. For readers drawn to tales of psychological suspense and supernatural danger, *LIT* is a compelling entry-point to what promises to be a thrilling series.

With its unique premise, layered storytelling, and strong characters, *LIT* proves Mark Anthony has crafted more than a typical genre novel—it's a thought-provoking exploration of human fragility and resilience. Highly recommended for fans of dark fantasy and horror alike.

NOVEL • STORY • LITERATURE   EDITOR'S CHOICE

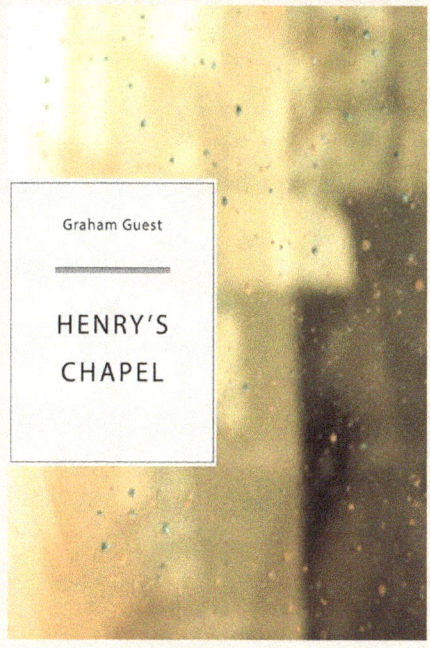
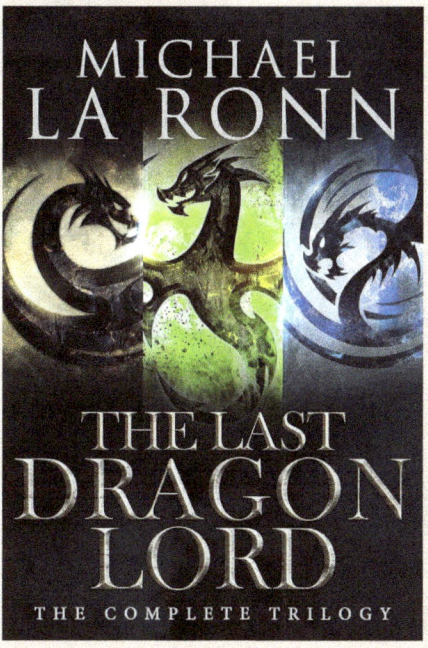
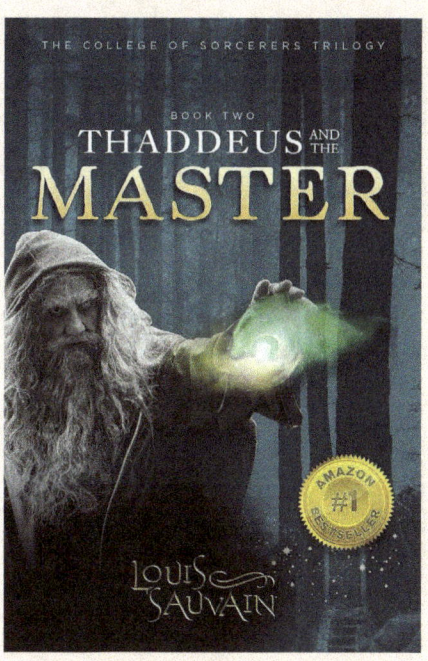

HENRY'S CHAPEL
by Graham Guest

THE LAST DRAGON LORD
by Michael La Ronn

THADDEUS AND THE MASTER
by Louis Sauvain

Innovative, intellectually daring, and structurally ambitious, Henry's Chapel challenges conventional storytelling with its unique metafictional approach and thought-provoking narrative framework.

A masterfully written dark fantasy, The Last Dragon Lord captivates with its rich world-building, complex antihero, and gripping tension.

Rich world-building, compelling characters, imaginative challenges, and heartfelt camaraderie make Thaddeus and the Master an enthralling fantasy masterpiece.

Graham Guest's *Henry's Chapel* is an ambitious, metafictional experiment that, while intellectually intriguing, ultimately falls short in delivering a compelling reading experience. The novel presents itself as an ana

lysis of Albarb Noella's fictional film, Lawnmower of a Jealous God, narrated through a character who provides a running commentary rather than a traditional storytelling approach. This unconventional structure has the potential to be thought-provoking, but it often becomes an exercise in self-indulgence rather than an engaging literary work.

At its core, the book grapples with deeply unsettling themes—incest, abuse, mental illness, and eventual liberation—set within a rural East Texas family. However, rather than allowing the narrative to unfold organically, Guest chooses to filter everything through an analytical lens, distancing the reader from any emotional engagement with the characters. The novel's exploration of storytelling, meaning, and the blurred lines between observer and subject could have been a rich terrain for metafiction, but it often feels more like an academic exercise than a novel meant to be read for enjoyment.

While some readers may appreciate its intellectual ambition and experimental nature, *Henry's Chapel* lacks the narrative momentum and emotional depth needed to make its themes resonate. Instead of drawing the reader in, its layered structure creates an unnecessary barrier, leaving it cold and inaccessible. For those who enjoy metafictional complexity, it may hold some merit, but for most readers, it is likely to be an exhausting rather than enlightening experience.

Michael La Ronn's *The Last Dragon Lord: The Complete Trilogy* is a masterful work of dark fantasy that delivers a compelling tale told from a unique perspective. The boxed set, containing all three books, offers a seamless journey into the blood-soaked, treasure-filled world of Old Dark—a supreme dragon lord whose reign has terrorised humanity for two centuries.

Unlike traditional fantasy heroes, Dark is unapologetically wicked, ruling with brute force and hoarding magic to elevate himself to near-god-like status. La Ronn boldly places readers inside the mind of a dragon protagonist, showcasing his ruthless approach to power and his calculated battles against betrayal. The intrigue heightens when a conspiracy emerges from within his own ranks, threatening Dark's dominion and forcing him to confront enemies who are equally devious.

The trilogy's strength lies in its characterisation and rich world-building. The narrative is unapologetically dark, yet fascinating, as readers are invited to witness the motivations and machinations of a character who doesn't fit the typical mould of hero or villain. Fans of the Age of Fire series or Tolkien's Smaug will revel in the gripping examination of ambition, revenge, and the nature of evil.

La Ronn's prose is sharp, and the pacing aligns perfectly with the high stakes of the tale. The trilogy captivates from its opening pages and doesn't let go until the very end. *The Last Dragon Lord* is an enthralling must-read for lovers of antihero narratives and dark fantasy epics. The Kindle edition's value-added format makes owning this masterpiece even more enticing.

Thaddeus and the Master, the second instalment of Louis Sauvain's College of Sorcerers trilogy, offers a thrilling continuation of the adventures from Thaddeus of Beewicke. Once again, Sauvain's mastery of world-building and knack for crafting compelling characters shine through in this gripping fantasy tale. Set against the backdrop of the College of Sorcerers, this story delves deeper into Thaddeus and his comrades' trials as they face an array of sinister obstacles and uncover growing mysteries.

Sauvain captivates readers with a rich tapestry of challenges, from evocative encounters with a half-mad centaur and sentient warrior statues to the shocking discovery of twisted motivations within the College's Faculty. The stakes are both personal and grand, with the school's Daemon and the enigmatic Pale Horse of Death casting ominous shadows over Thaddeus's fate. While the novel is packed with action, it also thrives on its themes of friendship, perseverance, and trust, as the brother Apprentices navigate the complex hierarchy and prejudices of their magical education.

For fantasy enthusiasts, the vivid world-building is a true highlight. The novel seamlessly balances dangerous adventure with quieter moments of camaraderie and self-discovery, offering a multifaceted reading experience. While it is recommended to read the trilogy in order, this book stands strong as a richly layered fantasy brimming with intrigue.

Thaddeus and the Master is a tale sure to enchant young adult readers, but its depth and wit will resonate with mature audiences as well. Sauvain's storytelling guarantees a page-turner that lingers in the imagination long after the last word.

EDITOR'S CHOICE

NOVEL • STORY • LITERATURE

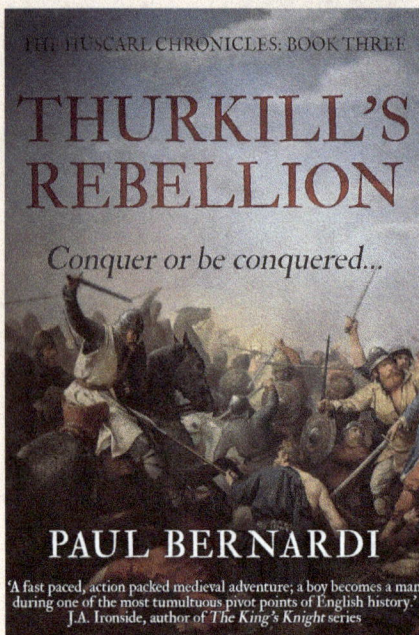
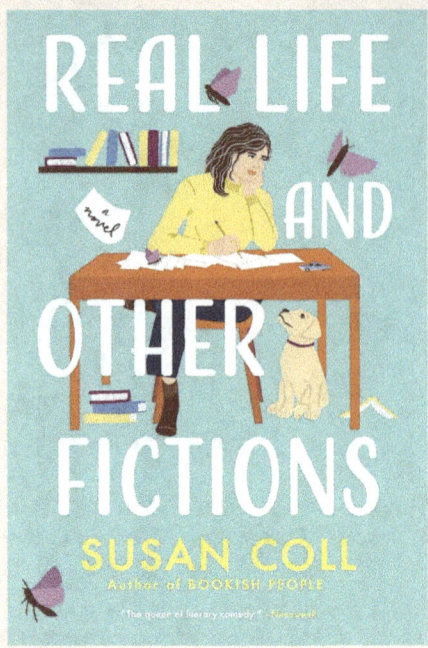

PLAGUED LANDS
by Nikki Brooke

THURKILL'S REBELLION
by Paul Bernardi

REAL LIFE AND OTHER FICTIONS
by Susan Coll

Plagued Lands enthrals with its thrilling plot, heartfelt relationships, and a courageous heroine, making it an unmissable dystopian gem.

A gripping, action-packed historical adventure with rich detail, compelling characters, and intense battle scenes. A must-read for medieval fiction fans!

Witty, heartfelt, and wonderfully eccentric—Real Life and Other Fictions is a captivating blend of mystery, humour, and self-discovery.

Nikki Brooke's *Plagued Lands* offers a gripping exploration of survival, trust, and resilience in a vividly imagined dystopian world. Set in a future where humanity clings to glass-enclosed cities to avoid ravaging diseases, the story powerfully captures themes of family bonds and the cost of safety when steeped in fear.

Martina, a determined and complex protagonist, anchors the narrative with her relentless courage and fierce devotion to her younger brother. Her struggle to provide for him amidst rising medication costs adds a palpable tension that resonates deeply, especially in light of contemporary issues around healthcare and inequality. The mystery begins when she witnesses someone outside the bubble, upending her understanding of the world she thought she knew. This pivotal moment sets in motion a fast-paced quest for truth that will keep readers on edge.

The supporting characters shine in their own right. Nathan, the enigmatic nomad, and Persephone, the driven pharmacy student, offer a dynamic mix of romance, camaraderie, and intellectual resolve. Their interactions with Martina provide moments of warmth amidst the bleakness of their reality. At its heart, the story asks what we are willing to sacrifice to protect those we love and what lengths we'll go to uncover the truth.

Brooke's prose is accessible yet evocative, drawing readers into a world that feels both foreign and unnervingly close to home. With suspense and heart in equal measure, *Plagued Lands* is a standout YA dystopian novel that will leave readers eager for a sequel. Highly recommended for fans of *The Hunger Games* and *The Maze Runner*.

Paul Bernardi's *Thurkill's Rebellion*, the third and final instalment of The Huscarl Chronicles, delivers a thrilling and immersive conclusion to this gripping historical saga. Set against the brutal backdrop of post-Conquest England, the novel follows the hardened yet honourable Saxon warrior, Thurkill, as he navigates a world where loyalty is both a virtue and a curse.

Forced into exile after avenging his slain lord, Thurkill's journey takes him to the borderlands of England and Wales, where tensions between the Saxons and their Norman overlords remain volatile. Yet even as he seeks safety for his pregnant wife and loyal comrades, he is inevitably drawn back into the fight for England's future. When whispers of rebellion arise, Thurkill sees an opportunity not only to battle the Normans once more but also to redeem himself for past failures.

Bernardi's meticulous research and eye for historical authenticity shine throughout the novel. The battle sequences are ferocious and visceral, plunging the reader straight into the heart of medieval warfare. Thurkill himself is a compelling protagonist—hardened by loss, yet steadfast in his convictions. The supporting cast is equally well-drawn, each playing a vital role in the unfolding drama.

Fast-paced and action-packed, *Thurkill's Rebellion* is a masterful blend of history and fiction. Fans of Bernard Cornwell and Matthew Harffy will find much to admire in Bernardi's storytelling. A worthy and satisfying conclusion to an unforgettable trilogy.

Susan Coll's *Real Life and Other Fictions* is a delightfully offbeat novel that blends mystery, satire, and self-discovery with an irresistible dose of cryptozoology. At its heart is Cassie Klein, a woman in her fifties whose life has been defined by an unresolved tragedy—her parents' deaths in a West Virginia bridge collapse when she was just two years old. Now, reeling from personal disappointments, including a failed journalism career and an unfaithful husband, Cassie embarks on a road trip fuelled by impulse and curiosity. With only her puppy for company, she sets out to uncover the truth behind her parents' fate, a journey that leads her to a peculiar cryptozoologist and the shadowy legend of the Mothman.

Coll's writing is sharp, witty, and rich with wry humour. Cassie is an engaging protagonist—self-deprecating, intelligent, and wonderfully flawed. Her existential crisis unfolds in a narrative that seamlessly intertwines the absurd and the heartfelt, making the novel both hilarious and deeply poignant. The book's satirical edge is particularly biting when it explores internet culture, failed ambition, and the fluidity of truth in storytelling.

While the novel's eccentric plot may not be for everyone, those who enjoy quirky, genre-blurring fiction will find it immensely rewarding. The blend of myth, mystery, and midlife reinvention makes for an entertaining and thought-provoking read. *Real Life and Other Fictions* is ultimately a story about searching for meaning in a world that often refuses to make sense.

NOVEL • STORY • LITERATURE   EDITOR'S CHOICE

UNAUTHORED LETTERS
by Tara C. Allred

THE MOVING BLADE
by Michael Pronko

MY AFRORICAN STATE OF SOUL
by Lucas Rivera

A gripping, emotionally rich psychological thriller with masterful storytelling, compelling characters, and an unpredictable mystery that keeps readers enthralled until the end.

A gripping, atmospheric thriller with rich cultural depth, sharp plotting, and compelling characters. The Moving Blade is a masterfully crafted crime novel.

A powerful, poetic masterpiece—raw, rhythmic, and deeply moving. Rivera's voice resonates with authenticity, bridging generations through identity, struggle, and art.

Tara C. Allred's *UnAuthored Letters*, the second instalment in the John Sanders series, is a gripping psychological suspense novel that delves into trauma, trust, and the fragility of the mind. The story follows Dr John Sanders and his former patient, Rebecca Brownell, who, after years of hardship, finally has a chance at a normal life. But her newfound stability is shaken when unsettling letters begin arriving—letters from someone who knows far too much about her past.

Allred's narrative is both deeply personal and profoundly suspenseful, weaving an intricate psychological web that keeps the reader on edge. Rebecca's journey, from institutionalisation to independence, is depicted with sensitivity, making her a compelling protagonist. While John serves as the rational anchor of the story, it is Rebecca's struggle with her past and the ominous threats against her sanity that truly drive the novel.

What sets UnAuthored Letters apart is its rich character development and immersive storytelling. The novel is not just about mystery and intrigue—it is a poignant exploration of mental illness, redemption, and the power of human resilience. Allred's prose is evocative, her dialogue natural, and her depiction of psychological conflict strikingly authentic.

The pacing builds masterfully, culminating in a chilling and unpredictable climax. While the mystery itself may seem straightforward, it is the emotional depth and character dynamics that make this novel a standout. *UnAuthored Letters* is an intelligent, emotionally charged thriller that will linger in the reader's mind long after the final page.

Michael Pronko's *The Moving Blade* is a taut and atmospheric thriller that immerses readers in the complexities of Tokyo's political undercurrents and cultural tensions. The second book in the Detective Hiroshi series, it builds on its predecessor with a gripping murder investigation that extends far beyond a simple crime.

When Bernard Mattson, a top American diplomat, is brutally killed, Detective Hiroshi Shimizu is drawn into a case that is as political as it is personal. Mattson's daughter, Jamie, returns to Japan searching for answers, only to find herself entangled in a dangerous game of deceit and conspiracy. Hiroshi, usually more comfortable in financial crime analysis than street-level investigations, must navigate Tokyo's labyrinthine political world, aided by his formidable ex-sumo wrestler colleague, Sakaguchi.

Pronko's deep understanding of Japanese culture and society adds an authentic layer to the novel. The settings, from dimly lit back-alley bars to the corridors of power, feel vivid and lived-in, creating an immersive experience for the reader. The pace is steady but builds toward a satisfying and intense climax, keeping the tension high without resorting to unnecessary theatrics.

What sets *The Moving Blade* apart is its balance of action, intrigue, and cultural exploration. Pronko crafts a story that is as much about the inner conflicts of its characters as it is about solving a murder. Fans of intelligent, well-researched crime fiction will find plenty to enjoy here.

A compelling and atmospheric read, this is a worthy addition to the *Detective Hiroshi* series and a strong recommendation for those who appreciate crime fiction with depth.

Lucas Rivera's *My AfroRican State of Soul* is a powerful and deeply personal exploration of identity, resilience, and artistic expression. Blending narrative nonfiction with poetry, Rivera crafts a decades-spanning journey that resonates with those who have experienced the intersection of culture, struggle, and self-discovery.

Rooted in the vibrant Afro-Puerto Rican literary tradition of Piri Thomas and Pedro Pietri, Rivera's work maintains the raw honesty and unfiltered emotion of his predecessors while incorporating contemporary lyricism. His words pulse with rhythm, carrying the weight of history, yet remain fluid and fresh, engaging both longtime hip-hop enthusiasts and a new generation of creatives.

The book's strength lies in its ability to weave personal experience with broader cultural themes—migration, racial identity, love, and faith. Rivera does not shy away from difficult truths, nor does he offer easy resolutions. Instead, he invites the reader into his world, allowing them to feel the intensity of his journey towards healing and self-acceptance.

Awarded the Literary Titan Book Award in 2024, *My AfroRican State of Soul* is more than a book; it is a living testament to the power of storytelling. Rivera's voice is both poetic and revolutionary, making this a must-read for anyone who values literature that challenges, inspires, and moves. Whether you are drawn to its historical depth, lyrical beauty, or raw authenticity, this book will leave a lasting impression.

USA TODAY BESTSELLING AUTHOR

A Journey Through The Mystical And Emotional

KIKI HOWELL
Weaves Magic and Emotion into Her Enchanting Stories

as told to Dan Peters

Kiki Howell shares insights into her career, inspirations, and paranormal storytelling, blending shamanic energy work, historical legends, and emotional depth to create unforgettable worlds while inspiring readers with her authentic voice.

Kiki Howell embodies the very essence of a storyteller, weaving magic and emotion into every word she writes. Her career, marked by the publication of over fifty stories and her rise to USA Today Bestselling Author status, is a testament to her dedication, skill, and creativity. From tales of gothic intrigue to her explorations of witchcraft and paranormal realms, Kiki's narratives captivate, inspire, and transport readers into otherworldly yet profoundly relatable experiences.

Her novel *Torn Asunder*, which earned her recognition at the Ohioana Book Festival, and her genre-spanning books, continuously climbing Amazon's Top 100 Bestsellers Lists, reflect both her versatility and the depth of her storytelling. Titles like *Hidden Salem*, rooted in historical legend blended with her own extraordinary encounters, and her works within the paranormal and occult genres, showcase her uncanny ability to balance intricate research with her intuitive artistry. It's no surprise that her books have captured the hearts of readers, immersing them in stories alive with vivid descriptions, authentic emotions, and meticulous attention to detail.

Beyond her literary achievements, Kiki's life is a mosaic of passionate pursuits. As a Shamanic Witch certified in metaphysical healing, a yoga teacher, and a creator of her own tarot deck, her wisdom and experiences find their way into her plots. Her ability to transform her personal truths—whether through shamanic journeys or reflections on motherhood—into compelling fiction sets her apart as a writer unafraid to merge the mystical with the deeply human.

In this issue's Star Interview, Kiki shares the inspirations and experiences that shape her extraordinary work. From her spiritual journey to her exploration of diverse genres, each conversation reveals the heart of an author committed to crafting stories that resonate and heal. She is a beacon of creativity, whose words are as captivating as her spirit is inspirational. Prepare to be enchanted as we delve into the world of Kiki Howell—where magic, love, and authenticity collide to create something truly unforgettable.

What initially inspired you to weave magic and paranormal elements into your storytelling?

Growing up, I was drawn to magical tales and supernatural lore. As an aspiring author though, research for my books gave me an excuse to buy non-fiction books on pagan/occult themes without having to come clean about my own gifts and magickal interests before I was ready. Now that I practice myself, energy work in many forms, I weave what speaks to me into my stories. Writing in paranormal worlds grants me an amount of fantastical freedom and control, to be able to create worlds and guide my characters through lessons in them without fear in a way I can't within the real world.

How has your background in Shamanic Energy Work and metaphysical healing influenced your characters and plotlines?

In a big way! I am a life-long learner, and what I practice, what I learn, what I am thinking about makes it into my books. Right now I am working on a fictional story inspired by the journals I've kept of my shamanic journeys. I'm all about writing what you know, turning truth into fiction.

Continued *on page 30*

STAR INTERVIEW

" USA Today Bestselling Author Kiki Howell, whose stories weave magic and emotion, graces our cover with her enchanting presence.

← Continued from page 28

STAR INTERVIEW

Kiki Howell's *Hidden Salem* is a spellbinding start to the *Salem Series*, masterfully blending paranormal intrigue, historical mystery, and a touch of romance. As an Amazon Top 100 Bestseller, this novel takes readers on a journey into the heart of Witch City, where history and magic collide in unexpected and thrilling ways.

The story follows Makayla, a journalist with empathic gifts, whose arrival in Salem leads her into a whirlwind of danger, self-discovery, and supernatural encounters. Howell does a fantastic job of capturing Salem's atmospheric charm, weaving rich details with an intuitive grasp of its historical and mystical legacy. Makayla's journey, from diving into local legends to confronting dark forces, is both engaging and layered with suspense.

The relationships in the story shine, particularly Makayla's connection with Noah, a protective and appealing local cop, and Lauri, a witch who becomes her guide in understanding her gifts. The love triangle element adds a romantic touch amidst the tension, though it never overshadows the gripping central narrative. The danger introduced by the dark coven ramps up the stakes, propelling the plot forward at a heart-racing pace.

Howell's vivid descriptions and keen attention to emotional depth make *Hidden Salem* immersive and entertaining, though at times the story's complexity can feel slightly overwhelming. Nonetheless, it's a minor flaw in an otherwise captivating read.

For fans of paranormal fiction and witchcraft-themed tales, *Hidden Salem* is a must-read. Kiki Howell delivers a thrilling and mystical tale that leaves readers eager to dive into the series' next instalment.

Hidden Salem explores both historical legend and modern-day witchcraft—what drew you to set this story in Salem, and how much research did it involve?

I felt called to visit Salem. Once I got there, the story unfolded for me in a series of residual hauntings and actual encounters with ghosts. While I did do quite a bit of research while there and once home, I would estimate that about sixty percent of the story is actually true, taken from my own experiences while visiting. Even the meals included in the story are ones I ate while there. That said, the dark coven and sexy cop, those are pure fiction.

As someone who's been published across genres, from gothic fiction to erotica, how do you navigate such varied creative spaces?

It keeps my creativity fresh. When I experience writer's block, I simply switch up genres, or incorporate a new one. This came from a writing prompt in a book about writer's block that my husband bought me which said to write in a genre you are not comfortable with. Hence my explorations in erotica. In trying new genres, you remove expectations, quiet the little voice inside your head who thinks she knows too much and overthinks everything.

You've spoken about taking a break to raise your children—how did motherhood reshape your perspective as a writer?

Being a mother motivated me to write, to continue on despite struggles and setbacks, in order to teach my sons to dream big. I wanted to teach them that they could do whatever they wanted to do no matter how big or how small if they only followed their heart.

Many of your books have reached the Amazon Top 100 in niche genres—what do you think resonates most with your readers?

I've been told many times that I can describe anything. Readers tell me that due to my descriptions, they can get lost in my books, feel like they are stepping into a place, practicing themselves, etc. In that vein, I often get compliments on my ability to describe emotions too, bringing readers close to my characters as well. I've also had several practitioners of magick compliment the research I do. One witch said to me that she could use my novel as a spellbook, that each spell within it read like a how to. I simply love to play with words, and that draws my readers into my stories.

What was the experience like creating your own tarot deck, and how does it connect to your narrative work?

Overwhelming to say the least! When my guides first suggested I do so, showed me the deck within a journey, my first thought was, do you realize there are 78 cards in a deck? But once I got the artwork for them done, each were actual mixed media paintings I photographed, the writing part went much easier. I went card by card, reading books and online posts about each one. Then I took a deep breath and let my intuition write my version of the card. I write my novels the same way. I research and plot for months, and so by the time I sit down with my computer, the story practically writes itself.

The anthology We Go On carries a deeply emotional and charitable message—how did your involvement in this project come about?

My father is a Vietnam Veteran, and it has always bothered me how those men who gave so much serving their country never came home to the hero's welcome they deserved. My story within the anthology came from a story my father had shared with me. I work through things in my real life within my fiction, especially tough stories and lessons. So I got to do that with his story and honor his service and sacrifice at the same time all while giving other writers the opportunity to do the same.

> *Kiki's journey from aspiring author to USA Today Bestselling Author with over fifty published stories.*

Can you share a bit about what becoming a USA Today Bestselling Author meant to you?

When I was first trying to get published, I would say that all I wanted was for someone who had never met me to like one of my stories so much that they invested in it by publishing it. At that point, I never even let myself dream of hitting any bestsellers list. And yet, here I sit, so many blessings in my career. It was not just hitting USA Today, because sometimes I still have to pinch myself to believe that one. I have the privilege of remembering the first time I made an Amazon bestseller list and saw my cover next to a book cover by an author I admire. I've had the honor of having a beloved author write a cover quote for one of my novels. The list goes on and on, and I simply sit and marvel and count my blessings.

What advice would you offer to emerging authors who are seeking to blend the mystical with the emotional in their writing?

As far as the mystical, do your research. Read everything you can. Then don't be afraid to make it your own. Write the story in your heart, not the one you think others want to hear. Making it your own will make all the difference. As far as emotions, again read and research, but also people watch and become a great listener. Then, use what you know.

STAR INTERVIEW

"Write the story in your heart, not what you think others want—making it your own will make all the difference."
— **Kiki Howell**

KIKI HOWELL
USA TODAY BESTSELLING AUTHOR

Ever since she was young, Kiki Howell has loved to listen to a well-woven tale with real characters, inspired plots, and delightful resolutions. Kiki could spend hours lost in a book, and soon she knew that creating lives, loves, and losses with just words had to be the greatest thing that she could do. To that end, she pursued her study of literature and writing, earning a bachelor's degree in English. She has now had over fifty stories published and could not be more grateful to see her creations out in the real world.

"After a long break having my boys, I finally just had to write again. And, as soon as I gave the stories the space, they entered it. It's both awesome and humbling to find the words in my mind become characters on a page and create their lives."

In May, 2011, Kiki was chosen as an Ohioana Book Festival author for her novel, Torn Asunder. Since the fall of 2013, she's had several novels hit the Amazon Top 100 Bestsellers Lists in several categories like Paranormal, Suspense, Witch & Wizard Thrillers, Gothic Fiction, and Occult Horror. In October of 2017, Kiki hit the USA Today Bestsellers List for the first time.

In a different vein, Kiki is also a Shamanic Witch, certified in Shamanic Energy Work with the World Metaphysical Association and the Accreditation Council of Holistic Healers. She's also a yoga teacher with a passion for helping others find ways to love themselves into a more authentic life. As a former English teacher, she brings her love of reading into all she does, finding new and eclectic ways of pulling all she has learned into each and every practice. She's even created her own tarot deck and co-created an online workshop series called Becoming Sovereign. Visit her at https://pensight.com/x/kirsteinann for more information.

Kiki resides in the Midwest with her incredibly handsome and talented, singer/songwriter husband and two children. When she is not writing, she is spending time with her family, reading, hiking, watching tv, or knitting.

The creation of her own tarot deck as an intuitive, artistic endeavour.

Hidden Salem inspired by real experiences in Salem, blending historical legend and modern witchcraft.

Insights into balancing motherhood and a writing career with inspiration for aspiring authors.

Reader's House || 45

LITERATURE

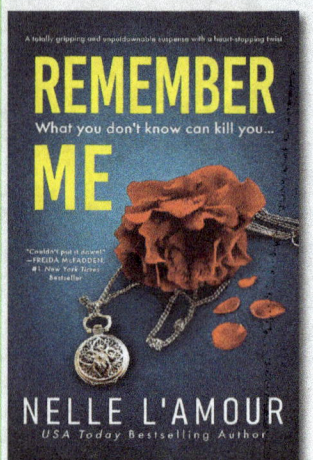

Crafting Engaging Stories and Complex Characters

Nelle L'Amour Weaves Passion, Humour, and Depth Into Unforgettable Romance and Suspense

Nelle L'Amour, a bestselling author of romance and suspense, discusses her writing journey, character development, and how she keeps readers captivated with emotionally charged stories that balance heat, humour, and heart.

"Remember Me," by Nelle L'Amour is a spellbinding suspense novel that grips you from the first page. With a thrilling plot, deep secrets, and unexpected twists, it keeps readers on edge. The characters are compelling and the gripping narrative makes it impossible to put down. A must-read for mystery lovers craving a heart-stopping twist. Highly recommended!

By MOSAIC DIGEST STAFF

Nelle L'Amour has captivated readers worldwide with her unforgettable stories that blend passion, humour, and deeply emotional journeys. A New York Times and USA Today bestselling author with over thirty books to her name, she has established herself as a force in contemporary romance, romantic comedy, and romantic suspense. Under the pen name Nelle Lamarr, she ventures into psychological thrillers, showcasing her versatility as a storyteller.

With a background in the entertainment industry, including her pivotal role in developing and producing the first season of Power Rangers, she brings a sharp understanding of character development and narrative depth to her novels. Her alpha heroes, from the charismatic W. in That Man to the complex figures in Unforgettable, are more than just commanding figures—they possess vulnerability, humour, and a depth that makes them irresistible.

In this exclusive interview, she shares insights into her writing process, her evolution as an author, and how she keeps her devoted readers engaged. From balancing steam and substance to navigating the ever-changing landscape of romance fiction, Nelle L'Amour continues to shape the genre with stories that stay in the hearts of her readers long after the final page.

From Power Rangers to Romance – Your journey from a successful career in television, including being the supervising producer of the first season of the children's television phenomenon, Power Rangers, to becoming a bestselling romance author is fascinating. How did your background in storytelling and marketing influence your approach to writing steamy, emotionally charged love stories?

This is a great question. What I learned from co-developing, producing, and writing several episodes of Power Rangers is that a great story starts from character and should include heart and humor, in addition to action. It's heart and humor that make a story, be it children's action series or a steamy romance book emotionally charged love stories. And it's key to have multi-dimensional characters that the viewer—or reader—can get emotionally involved with and root for. Importantly, steamy scenes should be emotional as well and stem from character. Writing a novel, however, is a lot different than writing a script. Scripts are 99% dialogue. Novels have to paint the picture for the reader—show not tell. It's a lot harder.

Creating Unforgettable Alpha Heroes – Your male protagonists, from the unforgettable W. in That Man to the ruthless yet passionate characters in Unforgettable, have captivated readers. What key elements do you believe make the perfect alpha male in romance fiction?

Another great question! I believe that while Alpha heroes are commanding and in-control and often think with the thing between their legs, I think they also need to be vulnerable as well. For me, the ultimate and most endearing Alpha hero also has weaknesses, a good heart, and a sense of humor. They make mistakes and learn from them Those are the traits I've instilled in Blake Burns in my THAT MAN series and Brandon Taylor in my UNFORGETTABLE trilogy as well as in other romance novels I've written.

Balancing Steam and Substance – Your novels are known for their sizzling chemistry, but they also explore deep emotions and intense relationships. How do you strike the right balance between heat and heart in your storytelling?

For me heat is secondary to heart. My goal is to create engaging stories and characters. Heat should be character-driven and organic to the story rather than gratuitous. Over the years, I've written fewer and fewer sex scenes. My early THAT MAN series had numerous sex scenes whereas a more recent romance, JANE DEYRE, a contemporary retelling of Jane Eyre, only had two steamy scenes, which were significantly less explicit than those in THAT MAN and UNFORGETTABLE. When I first started writing steamy romances about 12 years ago, there was a demand for a lot steamy, graphic sex scenes. IMHO, new readers of romance want more angst and humor than explicit sex scenes.

The Power of Fan Engagement – Your books have built a dedicated readership, with fans eagerly awaiting your next release. What role do your readers play in shaping your stories, and how do you keep them engaged throughout your writing journey?

My readers are very important to me. I maintain an active Facebook Reader page, Nelle's Belles. Often on that page I offer sneak previews of upcoming books. I also ask my readers for book cover advice and sometimes to help me name a character. (They love doing that!) I encourage my readers to reach out to me with by messaging or emailing me. I always personally respond. As I tell my readers at the end of every newsletter: "Always remember, you are the reason I write."

The Ever-Evolving Romance Genre – Romance continues to evolve with changing trends and reader preferences. How do you stay ahead of the curve while maintaining your signature style, and what do you think the future holds for steamy contemporary romance?

This a thought-provoking question. I tend not to write books to market. I write the story I want to write and the best book I possibly can. My next romance, THE BELL RINGER, coming in Spring 2025, is a contemporary retelling of The Hunchback of Notre Dame I don't have a crystal ball but I see an uptick in small-town romances and romantasy. And angst-driven stories with younger characters (though I'd love to see more books featuring older men and women). At the end of the day, in this very

glutted world of romance books, the cream will rise.

THANK YOU SO MUCH FOR HAVING ME! I really enjoyed answering your questions and look forward to what the future will bring!

With over 350,000 books sold worldwide, Nelle L'Amour continues to enchant readers with compelling narratives, unforgettable characters, and a signature style that blends passion with deeply resonant storytelling.

My readers are very important to me—I always personally respond to their messages and value their input in my writing process."

Nelle L'Amour
USA TODAY'S BESTSELLING AUTHOR

Exploring Memory, Emotion And Nature In Every Stroke

Elizabeth Magill discusses her artistic inspirations, techniques, and concepts, including emotional landscapes, fluid textures, cognitive dissonance, silhouettes, and the influence of Northern Ireland's history on her creative process.

ELIZABETH MAGILL
Inspires New Perspectives Through Her Captivating Landscape Art

As told to Noah Davis

"Land and landscape became a way for me to convey scenic beauty alongside a darker geopolitical environment."

Elizabeth Magill stands as one of the most captivating voices in contemporary art today, an artist whose profound connection to landscape and memory has redefined how we engage with the natural world through painting. Magill's work is nothing short of poetic—a delicate yet haunting mediation between beauty and introspection, between the external world and the deeply personal. Her ability to blend the tangible and intangible speaks to her mastery of creating imagery that feels both familiar and otherworldly, drawing viewers into a space where nature and human emotion intertwine seamlessly.

What sets Magill apart is not just her technical prowess but her fearless inquiry into the nuances of landscape as a site of wonder, tension, and duality. Growing up in the Glens of Antrim in Northern Ireland—a region of serene beauty shadowed by the complex history of The Troubles—Magill embeds her canvases with layers of meaning, memory, and the ineffable traces of human presence. Her work often feels like a dream paused in motion, evoking a sense of cinematic elegance underscored by subtle discomfort. Through her innovative use of techniques, from fluid paint pourings to photographic overlays, she crafts rich, textured surfaces where light, atmosphere, and mood take on lives of their own.

Engaging Elizabeth Magill in conversation is to witness the mind of a true innovator—an artist unafraid to embrace contradiction and complexity. Her pursuit of balance, achieved through the juxtaposition of painterly beauty and deliberate disruption, mirrors the very landscapes she depicts: places that exist not just geographically but emotionally and psychologically. Magill's willingness to layer the ephemeral with the unyielding, the serene with the unsettling, results in works that leave a profound impact on all who encounter them. It is our great honor to feature her brilliance in this issue and to delve deeper into her creative process, inspirations, and the philosophies behind her breathtaking oeuvre.

Can you elaborate on how your upbringing in Northern Ireland influences the themes and landscapes depicted in your paintings?

Before moving to London in the 80's, I spent my early childhood growing up in a place of scenic beauty called the Glens of Antrim. But it was a period marked in history known as, The Troubles, a brutal conflict which lasted 30 years and still has some legacy today.

Over time the notion of land and subsequently landscape as subject matter became an important part of my practice. Obliquely my paintings made reference to my early upbringing, and painting landscape became a way for me to convey the visual scenic attractions alongside a darker geopolitical environment.

The term 'inscape' has been used to describe your work. How do you define this concept in relation to your artistic practice?

> *Elizabeth Magill's ability to seamlessly combine beauty, tension, and innovation showcases her unparalleled brilliance within contemporary landscape art.*

I think it's about allowing internal thoughts and impressions that affect me to be made external. A lot of my work is set in some sort of outdoor or outside location, maybe a view seen from afar. This distance is both visual and psychological as it gives me some sort of a removed position, perhaps creating a space to be able to think about things.

Your paintings often evoke a range of emotions, from cinematic beauty to eeriness. How do you balance these contrasting feelings in your work?

I like trying to arrive at a balance of opposites, by having some kind of painterly skill alongside surface disturbance or giving the work a kind of trashed appearance in connection to moments of beauty, so that both approaches can exist simultaneously on the picture plane.

Hopefully this gives my work a shift in perception. Like when it's viewed from a bit of a distance it can appear tranquil but up close the paint application and process can give it a different reading.

I also like the term cognitive dissonance, which means holding and allowing conflicting ideas to exist simultaneously.

The more unlikely the balance appears, or the more implied tension that gets created, then for me, the more the paining seems to work.

Can you describe the techniques you use to create the rich, layered textures in your paintings? How do you choose which methods to employ for a particular piece?

All works begin by applying layers of thinly diluted and fluidly poured oil paint onto a horizontally placed canvas…this pouring and drying process usually goes on for some time or until I see something that I can visually or emotionally connect with.

Lately and from my photographic archive I've been making large silkscreen stencils.

My images are then superimposed or screened on top of my pre- painted canvas. This is a relatively new approach which has enable me to incorporate my love of photography.

How do film and photography inform your artistic process, and in what ways do they shape your interpretation of landscapes?

For as long as I remember photography has been an integral part of my work.

I see the photographic image as a fixed entity, it's function within my painting is to introduce something solid and seemingly certain… as opposed to the unpredictable quality that is made from my fluid paint pourings. I guess it's this duality of intention, I mentioned earlier that intrigues me.

In your work, you often incorporate elements like silhouettes and distant human figures. What is the significance of these elements in relation to the viewer's experience of your landscapes?

Figures are introduced for compositional reasons, but they appear infrequently because they seem to command too much visual attention, this can be a distraction to the overall dimension of the canvas.

So, I tend to paint them in and then out all the time. But I feel the unpopulated look of my work, still has a strong sense of human presence anyway.

> *Elizabeth Magill's work is a masterful interplay of surreal landscapes and emotional depth, blending technical innovation with a profound psychological connection. In the attached piece, her signature silhouette of a tree anchors the composition amidst vibrant hues and fluid textures—a dynamic interplay of warmth and cool tones that evoke a sense of ethereal beauty. The inclusion of human figures, understated yet poignant, enhances the narrative by suggesting quiet reflection and harmony with nature. Her technique, involving poured paint and photographic overlays, creates layered textures that redefine traditional landscape art, bridging the ephemeral with the tangible. Magill's work meticulously balances tranquility and tension, inviting viewers into a dreamlike realm where personal memories and universal themes seamlessly converge, making her artistry unforgettable.*

Art & Culture

Exploring Migration, Belonging And Justice Through Multimedia Creations

> "The layering in my work reflects the complex interplay of traditions, languages, and experiences from moving across cultures."

CECILE CHONG

Cecile Chong Weaves Cultural Identity And Universal Themes In Her Multilayered Art

Cecile Chong's work blends her multicultural upbringing with universal themes of identity and belonging. Through diverse materials and mediums, her art creates dialogues around migration, history, and our interconnected humanity.

In the vibrant world of contemporary art, few voices resonate as powerfully as that of Sienna Martz. An internationally recognized sculptor and fiber artist, Sienna has carved a unique niche by intertwining traditional textile techniques with innovative material manipulation. Her commitment to sustainability shines through in every piece, as she artfully transforms plant-based, recycled, and upcycled materials into stunning works that challenge the norms of consumerism and the excesses of modern life. Each sculpture is not merely an object of beauty; it is a statement, a call to action, and a reflection of her deep-rooted ecological conscience.

Sienna's work has graced galleries and museums across the globe, from the bustling streets of New York City to the historic avenues of Rome. Her ability to engage with diverse audiences speaks to the universal themes of nature and sustainability that permeate her art. By merging aesthetic beauty with a gentle form of activism, she invites viewers to reconsider their relationship with the environment and the impact of their choices. As she continues to push the boundaries of her medium, Sienna Martz stands as a beacon of inspiration, reminding us that art can be both beautiful and transformative. In this exclusive interview with Mosaci Digest Magazine, we delve into the mind of this remarkable artist, exploring her creative process, her commitment to sustainability, and the profound messages woven into her work.

Sustainability is a key element in your work. How do you go about sourcing eco-friendly and upcycled materials for your sculptures, and how does this impact your creative process?

As an eco-conscious artist, sourcing materials is a dedicated practice in a world where

Cecile Chong's artwork masterfully blends intricate figures, foliage, and fluid watercolor backgrounds, creating a serene and nostalgic atmosphere. The delicate blue monochromatic illustrations of children and a woman evoke innocence and curiosity, harmonized with dreamy, textured washes of cream and blue hues. Overhanging leafy motifs frame the composition, enhancing its connection to nature. This piece balances timeless craftsmanship with an imaginative narrative, inviting the viewer into a tranquil, evocative moment that sparks feelings of wonder and reflection.

Cecile Chong's evocative artistry masterfully bridges cultural narratives, evoking humanity's shared essence with innovation, depth, and profound storytelling.

most readily available supplies are often unsustainable. Depending on the art piece, I love sourcing secondhand clothing and fabrics at local thrift stores. Beyond that, I scour the internet searching for the most sustainable alternatives to common materials like organic kapok fiber instead of polyester stuffing, organic cotton instead of conventional cotton, and bamboo felt instead of wool felt. The plant fibers I choose to work with are incredibly high-quality which elevates my work. When working with secondhand fabrics, often the variety of woven textures and color palettes that come together while I source these supplies will help dictate how the artwork comes to life.

Your sculptures explore the adaptability of nature while critiquing unsustainable practices, especially in the textile industry. How do you balance aesthetic beauty with activism in your pieces?

I like to describe my work as a gentle form of activism. The artist in me has a primal desire to create beautiful works of art relating to nature that are both inviting and inspiring. And the activist in me has the desire to use my artistic voice as a means to encourage a more sustainable and ethical world.

Your work has been exhibited globally, from Berlin to Seoul. How do you think your sculptures resonate with audiences across different cultures, particularly in relation to environmental consciousness?

My hope is that viewers will reimagine the role of art in society, positioning my work not just as an object of beauty but as a catalyst for cultural transformation and sustainable thinking. However, since my artwork does not always visually convey concerns about climate change, animal welfare, and overconsumption viewers may not always make these connections. But because my work mimics organic and abstract forms, my work inevitably provokes thought and a kinship with the natural world regardless of the audience because we, as humans, have an innate curiosity when it comes to the natural world.

You employ both traditional textile techniques and alternative material manipulation in your sculptures. Can you describe how you merge these techniques, and what drew you to explore fiber as your primary medium?

My training in fiber arts was generally rooted in contemporary, alternative exploration rather than traditional approaches. While I learned techniques such as machine sewing and fabric dying, my mentors encouraged me to think outside of tradition and develop my own techniques of sculpting with fibers. I've always been drawn to the softness of fibers and its forgiving nature. This medium has allowed me to explore my fascination with nature through an abstract and vibrant lens.

As an artist dedicated to challenging consumerism and excess, how do you navigate the commercial art world while staying true to your ecological principles?

As an artist emerging within a digital culture, I've found utilizing commercial art forms such as social media has tremendously helped me grow my profession. I've spent years establishing my Instagram account and as a result, I have a devoted community of fellow artists and collectors who can follow and support my artistic journey. This platform has allowed me to share my ecological principles and bring more awareness to issues such as climate change, the textile waste crisis, and so on.

Your works are often described as inspired by the geometry of biology. Can you elaborate on how the natural world informs the textures, shapes, and colors in your art?

I have a deep fascination with how cells and organisms are formed through patterns and replication. I often use the transformative power of replication of a single form to create my sculptural pieces – building, layering, and structuring my work into something unexpected and quite fascinating.

Challenging Consumerism through Sculptural Beauty

Photo by Joy Masi

> "I like to describe my work as a gentle form of activism."

SIENNA MARTZ

Art & Culture

Sienna Martz Creates Transformative Sculptures That Merge Sustainability And Beauty

Sienna Martz uses upcycled textiles and plant-based materials to create sculptures that blend environmental activism, natural beauty, and cultural transformation, showcasing sustainability's artistic potential on a global stage.

In the vibrant world of contemporary art, few voices resonate as powerfully as that of Sienna Martz. An internationally recognized sculptor and fiber artist, Sienna has carved a unique niche by intertwining traditional textile techniques with innovative material manipulation. Her commitment to sustainability shines through in every piece, as she artfully transforms plant-based, recycled, and upcycled materials into stunning works that challenge the norms of consumerism and the excesses of modern life. Each sculpture is not merely an object of beauty; it is a statement, a call to action, and a reflection of her deep-rooted ecological conscience.

Sienna's work has graced galleries and museums across the globe, from the bustling streets of New York City to the historic avenues of Rome. Her ability to engage with diverse audiences speaks to the universal themes of nature and sustainability that permeate her art. By merging aesthetic beauty with a gentle form of activism, she invites viewers to reconsider their relationship with the environment and the impact of their choices. As she continues to push the boundaries of her medium, Sienna Martz stands as a beacon of inspiration, reminding us that art can be both beautiful and transformative. In this exclusive interview with Mosaci Digest Magazine, we delve into the mind of this remarkable artist, exploring her creative process, her commitment to sustainability, and the profound messages woven into her work.

Sustainability is a key element in your work. How do you go about sourcing eco-friendly and upcycled materials for your sculptures, and how does this impact your creative process?

As an eco-conscious artist, sourcing materials is a dedicated practice in a world where

Sienna Martz's innovative sculptures beautifully merge nature-inspired aesthetics with ecological activism, spotlighting sustainability while redefining the artistic boundaries of fiber and alternative materials.

Sienna Martz's innovative sculptures captivate with their biomorphic shapes and vibrant colors. Using upcycled textiles and organic textures, her works blend sustainability with artistry, evoking curiosity and connection to nature. Displayed in a minimalist gallery space, her creations challenge consumers to rethink their environmental footprint while celebrating the tactile, transformative potential of traditional and contemporary fiber art.

most readily available supplies are often unsustainable. Depending on the art piece, I love sourcing secondhand clothing and fabrics at local thrift stores. Beyond that, I scour the internet searching for the most sustainable alternatives to common materials like organic kapok fiber instead of polyester stuffing, organic cotton instead of conventional cotton, and bamboo felt instead of wool felt. The plant fibers I choose to work with are incredibly high-quality which elevates my work. When working with secondhand fabrics, often the variety of woven textures and color palettes that come together while I source these supplies will help dictate how the artwork comes to life.

Your sculptures explore the adaptability of nature while critiquing unsustainable practices, especially in the textile industry. How do you balance aesthetic beauty with activism in your pieces?

I like to describe my work as a gentle form of activism. The artist in me has a primal desire to create beautiful works of art relating to nature that are both inviting and inspiring. And the activist in me has the desire to use my artistic voice as a means to encourage a more sustainable and ethical world.

Your work has been exhibited globally, from Berlin to Seoul. How do you think your sculptures resonate with audiences across different cultures, particularly in relation to environmental consciousness?

My hope is that viewers will reimagine the role of art in society, positioning my work not just as an object of beauty but as a catalyst for cultural transformation and sustainable thinking. However, since my artwork does not always visually convey concerns about climate change, animal welfare, and overconsumption viewers may not always make these connections. But because my work mimics organic and abstract forms, my work inevitably provokes thought and a kinship with the natural world regardless of the audience because we, as humans, have an innate curiosity when it comes to the natural world.

You employ both traditional textile techniques and alternative material manipulation in your sculptures. Can you describe how you merge these techniques, and what drew you to explore fiber as your primary medium?

My training in fiber arts was generally rooted in contemporary, alternative exploration rather than traditional approaches. While I learned techniques such as machine sewing and fabric dying, my mentors encouraged me to think outside of tradition and develop my own techniques of sculpting with fibers. I've always been drawn to the softness of fibers and its forgiving nature. This medium has allowed me to explore my fascination with nature through an abstract and vibrant lens.

As an artist dedicated to challenging consumerism and excess, how do you navigate the commercial art world while staying true to your ecological principles?

As an artist emerging within a digital culture, I've found utilizing commercial art forms such as social media has tremendously helped me grow my profession. I've spent years establishing my Instagram account and as a result, I have a devoted community of fellow artists and collectors who can follow and support my artistic journey. This platform has allowed me to share my ecological principles and bring more awareness to issues such as climate change, the textile waste crisis, and so on.

Your works are often described as inspired by the geometry of biology. Can you elaborate on how the natural world informs the textures, shapes, and colors in your art?

I have a deep fascination with how cells and organisms are formed through patterns and replication. I often use the transformative power of replication of a single form to create my sculptural pieces – building, layering, and structuring my work into something unexpected and quite fascinating.

> Dr Shirin Lakhani: A visionary pioneer redefining intimate health, wellness, and aesthetic medicine with compassion and cutting-edge expertise.

DR SHIRIN LAKHANI

Inspires Change in Wellness, Aesthetic Medicine, and Intimate Health

Dr Shirin Lakhani champions intimate health, aesthetic innovation, and patient education, advocating for regulation, natural results, and destigmatisation of sensitive topics through her medical expertise, personalised care, and regenerative treatments.

By Amber Wilson

Dr Shirin Lakhani stands as a beacon of brilliance and compassion in the ever-evolving realms of intimate health, wellness, and aesthetic medicine. A trailblazer with an unwavering commitment to improving lives, she has redefined the way we talk about sensitive yet essential topics such as menopause, vaginal health, and erectile dysfunction. Her efforts to destigmatise these conversations have not only helped thousands to regain confidence and vitality but have also reshaped societal attitudes. Whether championing menopause-friendly workplace policies or advocating for tighter regulations in the aesthetics industry, Dr Lakhani has consistently been at the forefront of pushing boundaries and inspiring change.

Dr Shirin Lakhani revolutionises intimate health and aesthetics with exceptional expertise, compassion, and a commitment to patient safety and empowerment.

Her unparalleled expertise is matched only by her ability to balance precision with artistry, empowering her patients to embrace their truest selves. From pioneering the use of regenerative medicine to training practitioners in innovative treatments such as the O Shot and Vampire Facial, Dr Lakhani is undoubtedly leading the way in combining science, beauty, and wellness. Beyond her medical achievements, she is a passionate educator, using platforms such as media appearances, public campaigns, and even her own authored works to empower individuals with knowledge. Dr Shirin Lakhani's influence not only highlights her as a trusted figure in the health and aesthetics world but also cements her as a true advocate for holistic, informed, and life-enhancing care. It is a privilege to spotlight her remarkable journey and groundbreaking insights in this issue of Beauty Prime.

Can you tell us about your journey into aesthetic medicine and what inspired you to bring your medical expertise to this field?

I began my medical career as an anaesthetist and then a GP, but I've always had a keen interest in regenerative medicine and the science of aging. Aesthetic medicine offered the perfect intersection of my expertise—combining medical knowledge with artistry to enhance confidence and well-being. I was particularly drawn to the ability to improve not only how patients look but also how they feel, both physically and emotionally. That's why I now focus on treatments that go beyond aesthetics, such as intimate health and regenerative therapies, which can have a profound impact on quality of life.

"Aesthetic treatments should enhance rather than alter."
– Dr Shirin Lakhani

As a strong advocate for greater regulation in the aesthetics industry, what changes do you hope to see implemented in the near future?

The lack of regulation in the UK's aesthetics industry is deeply concerning. Currently, non-medical practitioners can perform invasive treatments with little to no training, putting patient safety at risk. I strongly believe that only medical professionals should be administering aesthetic procedures. We need tighter legislation to ensure that practitioners are adequately trained, that treatments are carried out in safe environments, and that patients receive proper aftercare. I'd also like to see better public education so that people understand the risks of going to unqualified providers. That is why I am working with the JCCP to try and bring about changes in legislation.

"Education is key. I always take the time to explain treatments in detail, including benefits, risks, and realistic expectations."
– Dr Shirin Lakhani

Your approach focuses on achieving natural results tailored to each individual's needs. How do you strike the right balance between enhancing beauty and maintaining authenticity?

Aesthetic treatments should enhance rather than alter. My philosophy is all about working with a patient's unique features to bring out their best version of themselves. That's why I take a highly personalised approach—assessing facial proportions, skin health, and the aging process to recommend subtle, natural-lo-

Continued *on page 56*

oking treatments. I also prioritise regenerative medicine, which helps stimulate the body's natural healing processes, leading to more authentic and long-lasting results. It's about refinement, not transformation.

You are the UK Trainer for innovative treatments such as the O Shot and Vampire Facial. Could you explain the science behind these procedures and the benefits they offer?

Both the O Shot and Vampire Facial use Platelet-Rich Plasma (PRP) therapy, which harnesses the body's natural healing power. PRP is derived from a patient's own blood and is rich in growth factors that stimulate tissue regeneration.

The O Shot is a revolutionary treatment for women's intimate health. It can help with issues like vaginal dryness, low libido, and even stress incontinence by rejuvenating tissue and improving blood flow.

The Vampire Facial, on the other hand, is a skin-rejuvenation treatment that combines microneedling with PRP to boost collagen production, improve skin texture, and reduce fine lines.

Both work with the body's natural ability to repair and regenerate.

> *Aesthetic treatments should enhance rather than alter.*
>
> -Dr Shirin Lakhani

Congratulations on the success of your book about the P Shot! What inspired you to write it, and how do you think it contributes to raising awareness about this treatment?

Thank you! I wrote my book on the P Shot because I wanted to break the stigma around men's intimate health and educate people about the benefits of regenerative medicine. Erectile dysfunction, for example, is incredibly common, but many men suffer in silence due to embarrassment or lack of awareness about treatment options. The P Shot uses PRP to improve blood flow, tissue regeneration, and sensitivity—helping men regain confidence and intimacy without resorting to medication or invasive procedures. My goal with the book was to provide clear, science-backed information in a way that's accessible and empowering.

Staying updated on new developments is essential in your field. Are there any advancements or trends in aesthetic medicine that particularly excite you at present?

Regenerative medicine continues to be an exciting area, and I believe it's the future of aesthetics. Treatments that stimulate the body's natural healing processes—like exosome therapy, fractional microneedling, and PRP—are becoming more sophisticated and effective. I'm also closely following developments in biohacking and how lifestyle interventions can work alongside aesthetic treatments for optimal results. Another trend I'm excited about is the growing emphasis on holistic aging—not just treating lines and wrinkles but looking at overall well-being, hormone balance, and skin health in a more integrated way.

What advice would you offer to individuals considering an aesthetic treatment, especially when it comes to choosing the right practitioner?

Do your research! With the lack of regulation in the UK, it's crucial to ensure that the person performing your treatment is a qualified medical professional. Look for someone with proper training, experience, and a good reputation—ideally, a doctor, nurse, or dentist specializing in aesthetics. Always check before-and-after photos, ask about the products they use, and make sure they provide thorough consultations. A responsible practitioner will never rush you into a procedure and will always prioritise your safety and natural results.

Patient safety and informed decision-making are clearly important to you. How do you ensure that your patients feel confident and empowered when selecting a treatment?

Education is key. I always take the time to explain treatments in detail, including the benefits, risks, and realistic expectations. I encourage my patients to ask questions and never feel pressured into making a decision. Additionally, I believe in a holistic approach—understanding their concerns, lifestyle, and long-term goals to tailor the best treatment plan. By fostering an open, honest dialogue, I ensure that my patients feel confident, empowered, and in control of their choices.

More.
Longevity & Wellbeing

Indulge in a journey of health with our premium blends

DR IVONA IGERC
Pioneers Innovation In Aesthetic Medicine Through Technology And Regenerative Advancements

BY LYRA GREEN

Dr. Ivona Igerc is a name synonymous with excellence, innovation, and leadership in the field of regenerative anti-ageing and aesthetic medicine. With over two decades of experience, Dr. Igerc has established herself as a global authority, educator, and visionary in the ever-evolving world of aesthetics. Based in London, her influence extends far beyond borders, as she teaches and lectures across South East Asia, Europe, and even at the prestigious University of Beijing. Her groundbreaking contributions to the field have earned her numerous accolades, including the prestigious Innovation Award at the University of South Korea for her pioneering work in stem cell research.

Dr. Igerc's career is a testament to her relentless pursuit of excellence and her passion for advancing the field of aesthetic medicine. She has revolutionized non-surgical procedures, such as rhinoplasty and "killer jaw" treatments, using non-invasive techniques to naturally correct imperfections. Her innovative use of Botulinum toxin for calf and shoulder reshaping has set new standards in the industry. Beyond aesthetics, she has also championed the use of Botox for medical conditions such as migraines, temporomandibular disorders, gummy smiles, and bruxism, showcasing her versatility and commitment to improving patients' quality of life.

As a thought leader and educator, Dr. Igerc has lectured at numerous international conferences, organised workshops, and trained countless medical professionals in the art and science of anti-ageing and aesthetic

Dr. Ivona Igerc discusses the transformative role of technology in aesthetic medicine, emphasising Personalised treatments, regenerative advancements, and the integration of AI, robotics, and exosomes for natural, bespoke results.

medicine. Her contributions to academia are equally impressive, with a published book titled Face, numerous book chapters, and peer-reviewed scientific papers to her name. She has also played a pivotal role in the development of medical devices and skincare products, including her own innovative face cream, IvyNano. Her expertise in adipose-derived stem cells and her membership in expert panels worldwide further solidify her status as a trailblazer in the field.

In 2017, Dr. Igerc founded the Face Design Academy (FDA) to elevate training standards in aesthetic medicine. Her dedication to education and safety has made her a sought-after speaker at international conferences, where she shares her cutting-edge techniques and insights with surgeons and aesthetic practitioners. Her recent travels to countries such as Turkiye, China, Croatia, Hong Kong, India, and the Philippines underscore her global impact and commitment to advancing the field.

The Intersection of Technology and Aesthetics: Dr. Igerc's Vision

In a recent interview with Beauty Prime magazine, Dr. Igerc shared her thoughts on the transformative role of technology in aesthetic medicine. According to her, technology is becoming increasingly integrated into all aspects of medicine, including aesthetics. From robot-guided surgeries to AI-powered diagnostic tools, the possibilities are endless. Dr. Igerc highlighted the potential of 3D imaging, which allows for detailed analysis of the face and body, providing insights into skin quality, volume, wrinkles, pigmentation, and more. This technology enables practitioners to offer highly personalised consultations and treatments, ensuring optimal results for patients.

Dr. Igerc also emphasised the role of robotics in aesthetic procedures. Robots can inject with unparalleled precision and consistency, ensuring even product distribution and minimising the risk of human error. However, she is quick to point out that while technology can enhance precision, it cannot replace the artistry and creativity of a skilled injector. "Aesthetic medicine is as much an art as it is a science," she explains. "The ultimate personalised aesthetic touch depends on experience, an exquisite eye, and a refined taste in beauty—qualities that robots and AI cannot replicate."

Technological Advancements Transforming Aesthetic Medicine

Dr. Igerc has been at the forefront of technological advancements in aesthetic

"The future is in the hands of technology but must be strictly supervised by doctors to achieve the ultimate personalised aesthetic touch."
– Dr Ivona Igerc

medicine since the early days of her career. Her work with lasers, ultrasounds, and radiofrequency devices has yielded remarkable results in skin rejuvenation and resurfacing. She was part of the team that introduced Fotona 4D Ultimate Facial Rejuvenation to the Chinese market, showcasing her ability to identify and implement cutting-edge technologies.

One of the most exciting developments in recent years, according to Dr. Igerc, is the use of exosomes in regenerative medicine. These tiny, cell-derived vesicles have the potential to revolutionise anti-ageing treatments by stimulating collagen and elastin production. Dr. Igerc's new skincare line harnesses the power of plant-based exosomes, offering a safe and effective way to boost collagen and elastin through simple, at-home treatments. This innovation reflects her commitment to making advanced aesthetic solutions accessible to a wider audience.

Dr. Igerc also highlighted the growing importance of AI-powered skin analysis tools, which map skin concerns at a micro level and enable bespoke solutions tailored to individual needs. Additionally, advancements in genetic testing and DNA analysis are paving the way for highly personalised treatments, further blurring the line between science and art in aesthetic medicine.

The Future of Aesthetic Medicine: Personalised, Non-Invasive, and Technology-Driven

Looking ahead, Dr. Igerc envisions a future where aesthetic medicine is defined by personalisation, non-invasiveness, and technological innovation. She believes that the era of overfilled faces is coming to an end, making way for bespoke treatments that enhance natural beauty. Biohacking, epigenetics, and hormone replacement therapy are also poised to play a significant role in the future of aesthetics, offering holistic solutions that improve both appearance and overall well-being.

Dr. Igerc's dedication to staying at the forefront of her field is evident in her approach to technology. She meticulously analyses and customises the settings of every device she uses, ensuring that each treatment is tailored to the unique needs of her patients. Her commitment to innovation and safety has earned her the trust and admiration of patients and peers alike.

A Legacy of Excellence

Dr. Ivona Igerc's contributions to aesthetic medicine are nothing short of extraordinary. Her pioneering work, innovative techniques, and dedication to education have set new standards in the industry. As a leader, educator, and visionary, she continues to inspire and shape the future of aesthetic medicine. Her passion for combining technology with artistry ensures that her patients receive the highest level of care, resulting in natural, undetectable enhancements that celebrate individuality.

In a world where technology is rapidly transforming the landscape of medicine, Dr. Igerc stands as a beacon of innovation and excellence. Her work not only enhances beauty but also empowers individuals to feel confident and comfortable in their own skin. As the field of aesthetic medicine continues to evolve, one thing is certain: Dr. Ivona Igerc will remain at the forefront, leading the way with her unparalleled expertise and visionary approach.

Dr. Ivona Igerc, a global leader in aesthetic medicine, shares her expertise on innovation, technology, and personalised beauty solutions.

CHARMAINE CHOW
Elevates Modern Skincare With GetHarley's Visionary Blend Of Technology And Expertise

BY LYRA GREEN

Charmaine Chow is nothing short of an extraordinary visionary, redefining the skincare landscape with her brainchild, GetHarley. Armed with a solid foundation in Economics from the prestigious London School of Economics, Charmaine's career trajectory took her from the high-paced world of finance to the nuanced realm of beauty technology. Her professional journey, spanning illustrious firms like Morgan Stanley, KKR, and Goldman Sachs, equipped her with sharp analytical acumen and an innate ability to identify opportunities where others see challenges.

Yet, what sets Charmaine apart is her deeply personal connection to her work. Inspired by her own struggles with skincare and a desire for clarity in an industry riddled with noise, she built GetHarley—a groundbreaking platform bringing science, human expertise, and technology into a seamless, hyper-personalised skincare experience. Guiding consumers to optimal skin health by leveraging a curated network of top-tier practitioners, Charmaine has not only elevated the standard for patient care but also empowered experts to deliver tailored solutions with unparalleled ease.

In this exclusive interview, Charmaine shares her inspiring story, delves into the innovative core of GetHarley, and provides profound insights into entrepreneurship in the competitive health and beauty technology sector. Her forward-thinking approach to sustainability, diversity, and leveraging technology for personalisation exemplifies the responsible yet dynamic leadership needed in today's world. Join us as we explore the vision, grit, and brilliance of the trailblazer behind one of the most exciting developments in modern skincare.

With the rise of artificial intelligence and technology in skincare, how do you see GetHarley innovating further to improve

Charmaine Chow shares her entrepreneurial journey, her mission to revolutionise skincare with GetHarley, leveraging AI and human expertise, while championing sustainability, accessibility, diversity, and top-tier personalised care for global consumers.

the customer experience?

At GetHarley we pride ourselves in the ability to make things seamless for the practitioner and the patient at once, so we are leveraging AI to help with automating a lot of tasks and processes in the company to achieve that. That said, we think the ultimate luxury is having a human on the other side of the conversation, so we still want to keep a human-in-the-loop experience at all times.

"I craved a trusted voice to guide me through the thousands of options for my skin."
– Charmaine Chow

GetHarley connects skincare experts with consumers — how do you ensure the quality and reliability of your network of clinicians?

To acquire its network of clinicians, GetHarley actively recruits qualified aesthetic doctors, plastic surgeons, and dermatologists by reaching out to professionals in the field, likely through direct outreach, industry connections, and marketing efforts, allowing users to choose a clinician based on their expertise and availability on the platform, effectively building a large pool of practitioners to match with clients based on their specific skin concerns; users can also choose to be matched with a clinician based on their needs and preferences through the GetHarley platform.

"The ultimate luxury is having a human on the other side of the conversation."
– Charmaine Chow

What challenges did you encounter while raising funds, particularly the recent £40 million, and how did you persuade investors of GetHarley's potential?

In the short run the market is a voting machine, in the long run it is a weighing machine. Fundraising is hard, you have to navigate not only your business trajectory but also adapt to market gyrations. In the early days, people didn't understand the vision of bringing skincare experts into the skin health conversation, investors were mainly investing in a lot of direct-to-consumer brands that were scaling rapidly and marketing-led. So it took speaking to many investors for them to understand that our vision was not to bring more skincare products in to the market but to empower practitioners to help patients find just the right skin solution for them, at all moments of their life.

"Sustainability is something we will always be mindful of and will be strengthened as we grow."
– Charmaine Chow

Continued *on page 62*

Charmaine Chow, visionary Founder and CEO of GetHarley, championing accessible and personalised skin health through innovation, expertise, and passion.

PHOTO: *Unlock your best skin yet with GetHarley—a revolutionary platform crafted by visionary Charmaine Chow. Experience seamless skincare consultations that combine expert advice with personalized treatment plans, empowering you to achieve healthier skin with every product curated just for you. Discover the blend of technology and human expertise that sets a new standard in skincare.*

How do you balance promoting medical-grade skincare with keeping the platform accessible to the average consumer?

I think accessibility has many dimensions – information and ease of understanding, as well as price and factoring in your time. I think our practitioners' curation and education of just the right products, for each patient, makes navigating the minefield of information in the industry much easier and much more accessible. In terms of time, you can order products to your door within seconds, again making it more accessible and easier for the consumer. in terms of cost, actually if you invest in 3-5 good quality products and use them to the very last drop, we find that in the long run you spend less. Many consumers might purchase cheaper products over the counter, but find that the products don't work, and so it's a wasted purchase and a waste of money. In addition, you can book an online skin consultation for £40 with a skin professional via GetHarley, without having to leave your house. We believe this has made expert advice accessible for many people.

The skincare market is highly competitive — what sets GetHarley apart from other platforms and brands entering this space?

GetHarley is about helping you find the right products for your skin, not selling you products that you don't need. GetHarley is brand agnostic, so not tied to a particular brand, making it democratic for the practitioner to pick just the right products for each patient. We have a community of practitioners that are best in class in what they do and we are humbled by the opportunity to serve them on our platform and help them service their patients on their journeys to happier healthier skin.

As GetHarley expands globally, what strategies are you considering to address the diverse skincare needs of people from varying regions and ethnicities?

We already serve so many regions and ethnicities... all genders, skin types. We have shipped globally to patients for years. Our expansion plans are about building practitioner communities out of the UK, but because we already serve the world, we are set up to facilitate people from all walks of life. Our offering of over 500 skincare brands, means there is a brand and product range for everyone.

What role does sustainability play in your product curation and business operations, and how do you intend to strengthen this focus in the future?

With skincare experts curating the right products for their patients, patients get great results and so use them to the very last drop. There is therefore less waste compared to buying, trying and discarding (which is much of the beauty industry). GetHarley curated product regimes are posted out in eco-friendly, fully recyclable boxes, with minimal packaging and no bubble wrap.

At GetHarley we practise hybrid working, so people minimise their recruit and maximise productively. We work digitally, we don't print anything we don't absolutely have to print and we also donate the products we don't sell to charities.

Sustainability is something we will always be mindful of and will be strengthened as we grow.

How do you see technology shaping the future of skincare personalisation, and what is GetHarley's approach to staying ahead of the curve?

I think technology will play a huge part in shaping the future of the industry and in particular personalisation of skincare. At GetHarley, we leverage our proprietary technology and data to help our practitioners get feedback on what their patients like, dislike and we share benchmarks against the rest of the skincare industry so practitioners can utilise this information during their consultations and the creation of their treatment plans.

What key lessons have you learnt as an entrepreneur in the health and beauty technology sector that you'd like to share with aspiring business owners?

Dig deep and understand if what is compelling them to start a business is strong enough to go through all the hard work, rejections and challenges. I would also ask them to think through the problem they want to solve and whether it is something they are really bothered by, because you really have to be so enchanted by the problems, to come up with great solutions. I'd also say at some point you also really need to let go and play the quarterback role and hire people.

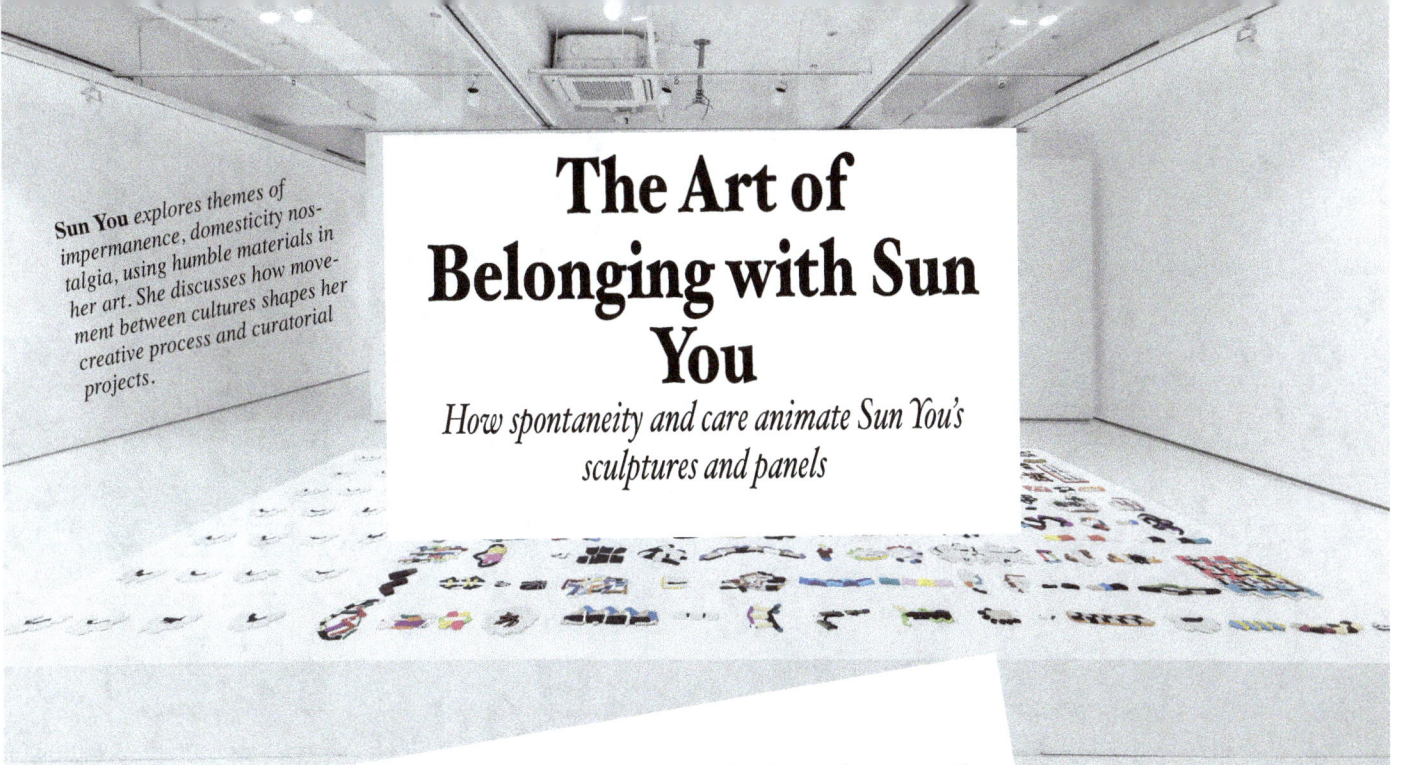

Sun You explores themes of impermanence, domesticity nostalgia, using humble materials in her art. She discusses how movement between cultures shapes her creative process and curatorial projects.

The Art of Belonging with Sun You

How spontaneity and care animate Sun You's sculptures and panels

Sun You's art embraces both resilience and fragility, transforming everyday materials into vibrant reflections on connection, memory interdependence.

Sun You's art offers a compelling meditation on themes of impermanence, interdependence play, bringing together the deeply personal with the universally relatable. Born in Seoul and based in New York, You has built an impressive body of work that transforms everyday materials like polymer clay and cardboard into intricate sculptures and wall pieces. Her thoughtful approach celebrates the beauty of fragility, creating pieces that evoke both lightness and resilience. Recognized with accolades such as the 2023 Contemporary Visual Art Award from the AHL Foundation, You's impact extends beyond her art. As a professor, curator director of President Clinton Projects, she is dedicated to fostering collaborative and supportive communities for artists.

Sun You discusses how her life between Seoul, Detroit New York has shaped her art, revealing the intimate themes of domesticity, nostalgia adaptation woven into her work. Her perspective brings fresh insight into the way movement, memory creative spontaneity guide her artistic practice, inviting viewers to reflect on their own experiences of home, transformation connection.

How has your experience of moving between different cities like Seoul, Detroit New York influenced your artistic process and the themes you explore in your work?

In my life, I have moved and traveled a lot. This fluidity and impermanence have influenced how I think and create. I prioritize flexibility and lightness. My work does not require fixed production sites, as it can be easily packed and made spontaneously.

How does the idea of function and arrangement in your process of packing art for transport contribute to the meaning of your sculptures?

My floor sculptures, made from polymer clay and cardboard boxes, have been exhibited since 2021. The form of these sculptures arises from a process in my work. I bake clay pieces in the kitchen oven and pack them in boxes to move to the studio. The arrangement of the clay is based on function: I organize them so they won't shift or break in transit. Whereas the paintings are composed with concerns like balance or movement, the compositions in the boxes come from a place of caretaking. There is a directness to this that I want to celebrate.

In your practice, you incorporate materials that are often associated with childhood and play, such as polymer clay. How do you see the relationship between these materials and the themes of domesticity and nostalgia in your work?

My abstract panels function as both paintings and wall reliefs. These works are made with polymer clay, acrylic paint wood. Polymer clay, one of my primary materials, is typically used in crafts such as bead making and children's play. The association with domesticity and baking in my work is reinforced through hand-building techniques, including rolling, pinching firing clay in my home oven.

For my show at Sardine in 2018, I created multi-panel paintings that are stacked on top of each other, with sculptural pieces inserted between the paintings. Both elements reflect a playful language reminiscent of children's play.

Several artists have inspired you. How do you think your artistic style and philosophy align or contrast with theirs?

I admire many artists, including B. Wurtz—we both use humble materials, embracing a slow, sublime succinct approach to gesture. I also admire Polly Apfelbaum, as we both are interested in creating provisional tableaus that celebrate women's work, history of craft the language of abstraction.

Can you elaborate on your thoughts about impermanence and interdependence, especially in the context of the current social climate and how it informs your artistic practice?

Impermanence and interdependence aren't ideas to me—they're facts. As a person, I try to embrace this and, as an artist, to materialize it. Some of the ways I do this include sculptures that are held together in precarious arrangements using magnets and gravity. Each time they're displayed, they shift and change.

As a curator, how do you choose the themes and artists for your projects what do you hope to communicate through these exhibitions?

My curatorial projects are often an extension of my interests as an artist and individual. These include themes such as artist migration and gentrification, feminism, physical flexibility in sculpture, intergenerational inspiration among artists more. These shows and events have been essential in fostering conversations and relationships that continue to shape my growth as an artist and educator. My goal is to bring people together, expand connections build community through artist-initiated exhibitions, projects curatorial opportunities.

Available in
PRINT

Americas to Australia

Europe to Africa Reader's House is available over 190 countries and thousands of retailers, platforms including Amazon, Barnes & Noble, Walmart, Waterstone's .....

ELECTRONIC

It is an electronic (flip book) format and interactive. Accessable from electronic devices like pc, smart phone, notepads..

ONLINE

All interviews, we conduct make them accessable online for free.

SOCIAL MEDIA

We are on Facebook, Instagram and X. Please follow us on social media
@readershousemag

contact us today for an interview opportunity at
editor@readershouse.co.uk

And so much more ...

Key Partnerships and Future Initiatives
Expanding the Boundaries of Authors and Books

Being featured in Reader's House means gaining visibility not just in print edition, but across the entire media spectrum in the US, UK, Europe and beyond

Key Media Partnerships:

- Associated Press (reaching 50%+ of global population)
- Benzinga (5M monthly visitors)
- Nexstar (68% U.S. TV household penetration)
- Major search engines: Google News, Google, Yahoo, Bing, Ask
- EIN Press Wire coverage
- NewYox Media magazines coverage (Mosaic Digest, Reader's House, CEO Vision, Beauty Prime...)

Broadcast & Digital Coverage:

- Major U.S. network affiliates
- 150+ million monthly radio website users
- 500+ UK media outlets
- Minimum 5 to 20 media placements per country (Albania to Zambia)
- Enhanced SEO positioning with quality backlinks from each media
- Optimized presence on e-commerce platforms)

Distribution Highlights:

- Available through major retailers including Amazon, Barnes & Noble, Walmart, Blackwells and Waterstones
- Available through local retailers Alaska to Wisconsin in the United States.
- Available in print LIFETIME
- Featured across 3000+ media platforms in the US, UK, Europe and beyond

contact us today for an interview opportunity at
editor@readershouse.co.uk